D0997167

FINER POINTS OF FLY FISHING FOR SALMON

FINER POINTS OF
FLY FISHING FOR SALMON

Neil Graesser

THE BOYDELL PRESS

First published 1989 by The Boydell Press, Woodbridge

The Boydell Press is an imprint of Boydell & Brewer Ltd
PO Box 9, Woodbridge, Suffolk IP12 3DF

ISBN 0 85115 522 7

British Library Cataloguing in Publication Data
Graesser, Neil, *1928–*
    Finer points of fly fishing for salmon
    1. Salmon. Angling – Manuals
    I. Title
    799.1'755
    ISBN 0-85115-522-7

The following sections of this book have been published previously in *Country Sport*: The Changing Scene of Salmon Flies, The Long Winged Variety, Wind, The Choice of a Salmon Fly, Fishing the Salmon Fly.

Printed and bound in Great Britain
by The Camelot Press PLC, Southampton

Contents

Introduction   7

CHAPTER 1. EQUIPMENT   21
            Rods   23
            Reels and Equipment   26
            Lines   29
            Casts   31

CHAPTER 2. FLIES   35
            The Changing Scene of Salmon Flies   37
            The Importance of Fly Size for Salmon   41
            Flies, Over or Under Dressed   44
            Salmon: What They Will Take   47
            Unusual Flies   50
            The Long Winged Variety   53

CHAPTER 3. CONTROL OF THE FLY   57
            Rod-Tip Control   59
            Handline Movement   64
            Short Line Fishing Technique   68
            Control of the Fly   71

CHAPTER 4. SALMON TAKING   77
            Salmon Behaviour Under Water Prior to Taking   79
            Upstream Taking   82
            Other Types of Take   85
            UDN and its Effect on Taking   90

CHAPTER 5. WEATHER CONDITIONS   93
            Dull, Cloudy Weather   95
            Bright Sunshine   98
            Wind   102
            Still, Quiet Weather   107

CHAPTER 6. WHEN TO FISH   111
            Before Breakfast   113
            Ordinary Daytime Hours   116
            In the Evening   121

CHAPTER 7. PLANNING A DAY   127
            The Choice of a Salmon Fly   129
            How to Cover a Beat to the Best Advantage   137
            At Which Side of the River to Fish   142
            Tide and Fish Movement   145
            Fishing the Salmon Fly   148

Introduction

I was born at Argoed Hall in the Llangollen Valley, where my father lived, in the late 1920s. I was the youngest son of a family consisting of five boys and one girl, and as the four eldest were boys there is little doubt that my parents had hoped that I might be a second daughter but that was not to be.

My father was an industrialist with several irons in the fire, and was a very conscientious business man. Although his main hobbies were shooting, fishing, golf and gardening, he never ever took a day off work to participate in these activities unless he was on holiday.

Argoed stood high above the river Dee on a bank of shale and gravel, with deciduous woodland cladding the bank between the house and the river. Above the house was the village of Froncysyllte (Pontysyllte) through which the main A.5 road passed, whilst across the river was the lush dairy farm of Plas yn Pentre in the foreground and a wonderful panoramic view of the vale of Llangollen with Crow castle and the edge of the Ruabon moor in the distance.

In the 1880s, the Welsh Dee had begun to erode the bank on which Argoed stood and after several minor landslips had occurred my grandfather decided to alter the course of the river in order to safeguard his property. At great expense he first built a small gauge railway straight down this steep bank to get the rocks into position, on the principle that the loaded trucks winched back the empty ones. Then he built a breakwater some 400 metres in length with rock fortifications on the river side at the head of it. It was finished off with a flat 4 feet wide walkway down its entire length. The operation was entirely successful, and as well as curing his erosion problem, he succeeded in creating one of the finest fishing pools in the river, naming it the Summerhouse Pool. To finish off his works he replaced the railway line with flights of steps arched with rambling roses, intersected at intervals by a red ash pathway, running straight down the bank from the side door of his house to the summer house at the head of the pool. In all there were seven flights of steps, totalling 232 steps in all; the red ash path, wide enough to take a large horse and cart, zig-zagged three times as it intersected the flights of steps on its winding descent to the river, ending up also at the summerhouse.

The Argoed beat on the Welsh Dee was some two miles in length from the Mill beside Plas yn Pentre farm house and buildings down-stream to the aqueduct which carried the Shropshire Union Canal over the valley. The centre of the beat, including most of the main pools, was all double bank fishing, but it only included the Plas yn Pentre side of the Mill pool at the top of the beat and the Argoed side from halfway down the Major Pool to the aqueduct at the bottom of the beat. Apart from the Summerhouse Pool, Run and head of the Major Pool, which were all open from one side or the other, the remaining pools were heavily lined with deciduous trees close to the bank or actually sited in a deciduous wood. It was due to this fact that pools such as the Mill, Pentre, Willow and New pool, were fished from a coracle, a much favoured mode of fishing on many other beats on this river, enclosed by similar woodland.

Although both my father and mother were keen fishers, my brothers and sister were not all that keen on the sport. I, however, from the earliest age was fanatical about fishing. So keen was I that it was a family joke that I had been born with a rod in my hand. Every spare moment of my childhood was spent near water, regardless of whether it was the goldfish pond, a burn or brook or (when accompanied) the river. Water, of any kind, seemed to have a fatal attraction to me. All I seemed to wish to do was to study fish, fish myself, or watch people fishing. My father, needless to say, was delighted and along with my mother did everything he possibly could to encourage me.

The same year that I was born, he purchased Rosehall Estate in Sutherland, including part of the river Cassley, from the Duke of Westminster, who was a great friend of my father. The family, in the early years of my life, used to move up to Rosehall in May for three weeks, when my elder brothers had gone back to school, and then again in early August until mid-September for the duration of the school holidays. My father used to come up for a week periodically, if business commitments allowed.

Rosehall was a fishing haven, not only because of the river but because the many burns in the neighbourhood abounded with trout and there was also a 5 acre man made lake, only fifty yards from the front door of the house, stocked annually with brown and rainbow trout from the MacNicol's hatchery at Ardgay. Needless to say, my father took every advantage of these facilities to cultivate my keen-ness on the sport, and in this he was ably supported by my mother, their friends, and the keeping staff of Rosehall and neighbouring estates.

From the age of three onwards, I was taken to the burns when these were in spate, with a bamboo cane and a length of line attached to which was a worm mounted on a Stewart tackle, and, of course, met with immediate success. Naturally, as a result I was hooked for evermore and from that moment of time onwards became a dedicated fisherman, spending every moment I could, both at Argoed and Rosehall, beside water. I always remember, even in my childhood at Rosehall that on Sundays when I was not even allowed to fish for trout, I would go to a burn, the lake or maybe the river, and just lie quietly beside a pool, literally for hours, watching fish movement and where they resided, fish fauna, or even the movement of water flowing quietly past me. As I grew older, I used to ply insects or worms, gleaned from underneath stones on the bank, on to the sur-face of the water, watching carefully how they were carried by the surface currents and the behaviour of fish and their movements as these objects came into their vision. Even at that early age, every-thing of interest was noted and remembered.

At Christmas 1931, Sandy Prentice, an old Edinburgh friend of my parents, had a 4 feet 6 inches spliced Greenheart rod specially made for me, and presented it to me complete with a reel and line to balance. At the same time, my father and an uncle completed the outfit by providing me with flies and hooks in a leather fly wallet. As a result, before my fourth birthday, I became proficient with this equip-ment and that summer was promoted from burn fishing to fly fishing either from a boat on the lake or Kyle, or bank fishing on the river, always accompanied by one of the long-suffering estate staff at Rosehall. That same year I caught brown and rainbow trout on the fly, and my first sea trout, albeit on a worm. The latter was my most prized, as it had sea lice and weighed 14 oz.

Sandy Prentice followed up his 1931 Christmas present the follow-ing year with a 7 foot spliced Greenheart rod, on which I killed my first salmon at the age of 6 years, and many years later in 1949 caught a 16½ lb seatrout on the Kyle, which I had to beach, as we had no landing net big enough to cope with it. This beautifully balanced little rod is still going strong and as well as helping to teach my two children, Hugo and Audrey, to fish, is used frequently by me when I go loch or Kyle fishing for trout, seatrout and salmon.

Looking back on my youth, fanatical as I was as a fisherman, I am sure this fervour could easily have waned if it were not for the kindly advice and gentle encouragement which I so readily received, not only from my parents and their fisherman friends, but also from the many experienced keepers and ghillies in whose capable hands I was placed from time to time. Their extreme patience and long-sufferance must have been tried to the extreme, when bombarded by quizzical questions by a precocious child. However, in spite of my age, at no time were they ever anything but courteous and helpful, always explaining in the minutest detail tips on how to improve my casting, how to present my flies in an attractive manner to my quarry, and many other basic facts about fly fishing. Certainly, on my behalf, I must admit they always had an avid and attentive pupil with an aptitude to listen and pick up these tips fairly quickly. In those days I was far from strong and did not enjoy the best of health, always being prone to chesty conditions as a result of simultaneous pneumonia and whooping cough when I was only 21 months old. I was also slightly built and even in my late teens was nick-named 'Gandhi' at school because of that fact. Therefore, I often tired quickly, but instead of wanting to go home I merely sat down and insisted that my companion fished, whilst I watched intently every move he made. Even to this day, I believe that I learned a tremendous amount from watching these experienced men fishing during my frequent rest periods – almost as much as I did from the actual tuition from these same people. Often, one picked up little quirks of rod movement or angle of rod which these men did automatically, but at the same time unconsciously, and because of this fact did not think it worth passing on to their pupil. Nevertheless, these minute details often proved to be vital to their success.

I must make a mention of two of these great ghillies, both really outstanding fishermen in their widely differing ways as well as being amongst the cream of nature's real gentlemen. Firstly, there was John Menzies, my father's head keeper and ghillie at Rosehall for over forty years. A tall, gaunt man with a wonderful weather-beaten complexion due to many years spent on the hill and the river, with a grey moustache and a wry mischievous smile. John was a man of impeccable character, and drew himself up as straight as a ramrod when he greeted anyone; he lived to the ripe old age of over ninety. His nickname, given him with awe by both tenants and guests of my father on the river was 'Another Yard', due entirely to the fact that whenever he accompanied them on the river he always asked them to cast out an extra yard of line, in order to reach the fish, simply because although the Cassley seems at first sight to be a small river, when it is in good order it requires on the whole extremely long distance casting to cover the fish properly. John was always renowned as a very strong spring fisherman and he always used a 16 foot Green heart rod, aptly named the barge pole, and favoured very large 9–10/$^{\circ}$ flies when other people were using 4–5/$^{\circ}$ sizes. It was quite remarkable how many times he was successful after several other people had fished a pool without result.

In his early years at Rosehall, he seldom fished after mid-April as he was too busy training dogs and killing vermin. Before coming to Rosehall he was employed on a very good spring beat on another river, and the wife of the owner became so angry at Menzies wiping her eye time after time with his big flies as he fished down the pools behind her, that she at last complained that he was ruining the pools by using them. Eventually the atmosphere became so tense between them that John decided to give in his notice, and duly left.

Secondly there was George Ross, the father of the present manager of the Lower Oykel Fishings. I spent many, many happy days with George, not only throughout my childhood but long afterwards right up to the time he died, unfortunately at far too young an age. Of all my many tutors I probably learnt more from this man than any of the rest both on the Oykel and also boat fishing on Loch Ailsh for trout and seatrout. George was a stockily built man, with a ruddy complexion and grey moustache, a good sense of humour and a delightful smile, quietly spoken with a very courteous manner. He was a great all-round fisherman and knew the Oykel river from top to bottom like the back of his hand, knowing exactly where to take you to give you the best chance during every season of the year, in any height of water. He was also a great lover of nature and extremely knowledgeable on the subject, so that even if fish were dour and difficult to catch, one never found the day long when George was one's companion because he always had something to discuss or some story to tell.

I always remember a day in late March on the Washing Pool with George. Fish were taking as freely as trout and after an hour or two I turned to George and said, 'This is more like slaughter than salmon fishing; I think I'll go home.' George looked at me in astonishment, and with a wry smile said, 'Keep at them sir, because many a time they make a d . . . . fool of you.'

For many years after I came up to manage Rosehall for my father, George and I had a friendly rivalry as to which river would catch the first fish of the season. It was a great sadness to me when George had a heart attack on the banks of the Oykel and died some time later after we all thought he was on his way to make a good recovery.

My early apprenticeship on the Welsh Dee was not such a success story as that at Rosehall, mainly because in those days on that river one was dealing with really heavy fish in the spring time. At Argoed, for the first month of season (15th March to 15th April) the average weight of the fish was nearly 20 lb. The native Dee fish were long, lanky, streamlined fish with large tails, which fought harder than any other fish I have ever come across in my long fishing career. It was for this reason that the first twenty-three fish I hooked on this river were lost as I simply did not have the strength or stamina to hold them on my small rod. However, the more I lost, the more determined I became to end up as winner one day and that was finally achieved when still at a very young age. Naturally, as I was born at Argoed, I had a great affection for the place and used to run down the steep flights of steps which led to the Summer House Pool whenever I had a spare moment to spend. If I was not able to fish myself, then I avidly watched those who were fishing, or lay quietly in the wood above the Major Pool watching the rows of fish lying close in against the cliff face below me, whilst on other occasions I would go up to the Pentre Pool and climb one of the trees from which I had a bird's eye view above the five tree lie at the head of the pool. From this position, I could watch and study the fish residing below me. All the time I was learning not only about salmon movement and where they lay in differing heights of water, and what depth in the water they lay at, but also about the composition of the bed of the river, pinpointing stones and rock ledges, shallow ridges, etc. At the same time, I was of course also able to study trout, grayling and other fish movement. All this precious information was listed and assimilated over many, many years and greatly helped my success rate as I became older and was able to fish more myself. By the time my family left Argoed, I practically knew every stone on the river bed and every lie where fish were likely to reside, in any height of water.

As I grew older, so my father ensured that I was fully ambidextrous in my casting ability and if he thought I was getting rusty with my right shoulder, then he forced me to fish from the Pas yn Pentre side so as to strengthen it. Sometimes I was not amused, but looking back on those days, I often thank him for his thoughtfulness. Luckily as it so happened, the home bank at Argoed was the right bank needing left hand casting, whilst at Rosehall the home bank on the Cassley was the left bank requiring right hand casting. Therefore, from a very early age both my shoulders were brought into action, but what he was really ensuring was that one shoulder did not become the master shoulder and get stronger than the other.

My main tutors on the Welsh Dee were, apart from my parents, Captain Hughes Parry of the Fechan; Mr Josh Denton, a tenant of my father's from Macclesfield; and our wonderful old coracle handler and ghillie, Robert Jones, who, although he knew all there was to know about fishing, strangely enough had never hooked or landed a salmon himself. All were responsible for teaching me the many varied methods of fly fishing, spinning and bait fishing, including mounting baits in their own differing ways, and all were extremely patient and kindly in their tuition.

During the latter part of my life at Argoed, Dr Jack Jones of Liverpool University and Mr King, the Fishery Officer, were very helpful when I was studying the life cycle of salmon and the conservation of the species. I was also lucky enough to spend many happy and interesting hours at Dr Jones's observation tank on the banks of the River Alwen, a tributary of the Dee, at Pont-Barcer. It was during these many visits that I gained a large part of my knowledge concerning the spawning cycle of these fish, as I was able to witness salmon spawning on several occasions through the armoured glass of the observation hut, virtually at eye level, when every detail was clearly visible.

On the Welsh Dee I was able to observe very clearly from certain vantage points both in the Major and Pentre Pools, the behaviour of fish when minnows, prawns, shrimps and worms were presented to them in the lower range of water flows and on many occasions could clearly see these fish as they actually took one of the varied lures, as well as observing their movement and behaviour in the water as the lure first came into their vision. This information has proved to be invaluable to me as a fisherman, and has undoubtedly been partially responsible for improving my success rate as an angler. Unfortunately, however, I was never able to find a place on the Argoed water where I was able to witness visually a salmon's behaviour when a fly came into its vision, nor did I ever get a really clear view on that river of a fish actually taking a fly. This was mainly because of the slight turbidity in the water when the optimum conditions for fly fishing prevailed, whereas when bait fishing was at its best the water was nearly always gin clear and, therefore, both the lure and the salmon lying in the pool were clearly visible from my observation points at all times.

However, when I moved up to Rosehall to manage the estate for my father in 1950, the opportunity to study salmon actually lying in pools and at the same time being able to watch my fly as it worked over them was readily afforded to me. This was because both on the Cassley and many other neighbouring rivers, there are an abundance of rocky gorges through which these rivers flow. Many main holding pools are set deep down in these gorges and it is, therefore, often necessary to fish some of these from rock ledges sited high above the water level in the pools. It is a common occurrence to be able to look down from these high stances, during the months of April and May

when the water is gin clear, and when the light is at the right angle one can see not only the fish lying in the pool but also every rock and detail of the bed of the river too. When one fishes a pool under these conditions, one is able to watch both the movement of the fly and the movement made by the fish simultaneously, and on numerous occasions I have watched my fly being taken by my quarry.

During nearly fifty years of experience of fishing these gorges, not only have I been able to build up a wealth of knowledge on how best to control my fly in all types of water flow and, therefore, how to present it to its best advantage, but I have also been able to glean priceless knowledge on the subject of how a salmon actually approaches and takes a fly, and more importantly, what the fish does immediately after having taken the fly over a wide range of differing water flows.

Through the same means, I have built up a tremendous amount of factual information as to which fish are most readily taken in a pool in regard to the position where they are actually lying in that pool, over a wide fluctuation of water flows. Experienced anglers will know that the pattern of where fish lie in renowned holding pools seldom varies from one year to another, and if they fish a river regularly they will know from experience in every height of water where fish are most likely to take in each individual pool. However, what is interesting from the knowledge I have built up on this subject is how this varies so tremendously when the pool is fished from the opposite side of the river. I have found that in these gorge pools seldom, if ever, does one catch fish in the same taking lie when the pool is fished from both banks but instead, from an entirely different lie. In other words, if fish take in a certain lie in a pool when this is fished from the right bank, then when the pool is fished from the left bank under similar conditions, fish in the same lie are virtually uncatchable. From my experience, it nearly always follows that the fly moving away from fish is more likely to attract them than the fly which is moving in towards them.

Quite apart from the points I have already stressed, the ability to look down into pools and visually see the composition of the river bed, fish lying in pools and where they lie, while at the same time be able to watch one's fly working and observe its actions as it encounters surface and underwater currents, is an invaluable aid to any angler. Tutors teaching beginners to fish will find it an asset to take their pupils to some high vantage point where they can fish from because they can then demonstrate clearly how they should be controlling their fly and point out their pupils' mistakes visually. In this way, even the complete beginner can be shown in a matter of minutes the simple

15

Fishing the Crow's Nest from the high ledge

rudiments of rod control, which is often more difficult for a beginner to master than the actual act of casting.

I know that I myself learned very quickly, entirely through being able to watch visually my fly traversing the width of the pool, the best means of being able not only to make it hesitate the moment it lands on the water on the far side of the pool but also how best to make it hang and hesitate over likely places on its traverse across the pool. I freely admit that it took quite some time before I achieved what I set out to do, and sometimes one has to use slight variations according to the type of water one is actually fishing, but these are all tips which are learnt entirely through experience. However, these are tips which I would never in the realms of fantasy have been aware of had I not had the opportunity to fish regularly from advantage points high above the pool I was fishing.

The only slight disadvantage that I have found from fishing on these high vantage points is the strike, because the amount of line which is hanging in the air between one's rod tip and where the line actually begins to cut the water is considerably longer than it would be when fishing from bank or water level, under normal conditions.

In fact, one really has to get into the bad habit sometimes of striking before one actually feels the fish, otherwise if one waits for the pull, the fish has often already ejected the fly by the time it comes. I freely admit that when I first began to fish from high vantage points I was mis-timing my strike more often than the times when I got it right, but very soon, through pure vision, I was able to see for myself what I was doing wrong and then cured that problem.

Another point of interest is the fact that the shorter the length of line one uses, the more control one has over it, and I have always found since I learned this technique that I now kill considerably more fish on a short line when fishing from bank level than I ever did before.

I now find that very often it pays handsome dividends to fish a wide pool down first with a short line, and then return to the head of the pool and fish it with the full length which is required to cover the whole of the pool and I am quite certain that by so doing I now kill more fish than by fishing the entire width of the pool in a single fishing.

Another advantage, of course, is to be able to see and study where fish lie in a pool, especially with regard to underwater rocks and ledges. Many times one will find that they favour in front of a rock just as much as they do behind it, and when there is an eddy or underwater obstruction diverting the current slightly sideways, it is

Fishing the neck of the Round Pool

A successful end to a day

interesting to note how fish alter the angle at which they are lying, in order to be facing direct into this current. The depth at which they lie in relation to the bed of the river is another point of great interest, and many may be surprised to find that often in low water temperatures they lie considerably nearer the surface than they do from the bed of the pool, and in the summer time when water temperatures warm up, they lie even higher in the water unless they are disturbed.

All the information gleaned visually as a result of fishing from a vantage point high above the water can be invaluable when an angler is fishing a beat or pool from the bank or water level. Not only will this enable him to read a pool to better advantage and recognise underwater lies more easily, which otherwise would have gone un-noticed, but it will also ensure that he is in better control of his fly at all times and enable him to concentrate his efforts more effectively on those parts of the pool he is fishing which are likely to prove to be most productive.

In this book I try to emphasise some of the points I have learnt, almost all of them from being fortunate enough to be able to spend many happy hours both studying fish and fishing from high stances, sometimes 30 feet or more above my pool. I have not the slightest doubt that this priceless experience has played a vital part in my success as an angler.

I only hope that some of these tips may prove to be as rewarding to others as they have been to me.

CHAPTER 1

EQUIPMENT

Rods

Once again, being of the old school I was taught to fish and brought up on wooden rods, spliced Greenheart and then more recently spliced split cane or the ferruled steel centred or ordinary cane rods. All of these were powerful heavy rods in the larger sizes, from 14–17 foot, and beautifully actioned easy to time rods in the medium, 11–13 foot 6 inch sizes.

Being a powerfully built man myself, I normally used Greenheart spliced rods with heavy zinc reels to balance them, and a No. 7 tapered kingfisher line in the spring time, whilst I used a variety of the same type of rod in the summer months, ranging from 12–13 foot 6 inches, according to the size of the river I was fishing. These old Greenhearts were slow-actioned rods with extreme power and capable of overcoming most adverse weather conditions with ease. Having no dead spot at all, due to the spliced joints, they literally worked the whole way from the cork handle right up to the rod tip, and were one of the smoothest types of rod I have ever handled.

The split cane rods with steel centres were also very powerful but on the whole heavier than the well-seasoned Greenheart, and needed a heavy reel on the butt to balance them, otherwise with a lot of weight forward they were very hard on the angler's wrists. These powerful rods had two dead spots, where the metal ferrule joined the centre piece to the butt and to the rod tip. With the friction of casting, faults often appeared above and below each joint and, therefore, the rod was likely to break at these places especially the older second-hand ones. Also, if these rods were not looked after and varnished and rebound regularly, water could get into the heart of the rod and rust begin to eat into the steel centre. If this happened, the rod was often finished, whereas if a spliced rod did break then one merely had a new piece made and the rod was as good as new.

Shortly after the war, a firm called Sharps began to manufacture spliced split-cane rods, and these were amongst the nicest actioned wooden rods I have ever used, especially in the 12–14 foot range. Although they also made 15–16 foot rods, these seemed to be on the whole softer actioned, and it was rare to get a good powerful rod in these sizes. From experience, I always used to choose rods of this make made of the darker grained cane, and found this tip served me well as the rods made of the lighter grained cane were not nearly so powerful, and often soft in the centre piece with no lifting power.

For a very short time at the end of the war, metal rods did appear on the market but these were horrible to cast with and impossible to time, as they were far too springy and whippy, catapulting the fly out of the water like a rocket on the back cast.

Once glass-fibre rods came on the market, everything was transformed and these powerful rods felt like a willow wand in the hands of we old stagers in comparison to the heavy wooden rods which we were so used to. From then on up to the present era, with carbon fibre and boron fibre, the whole ball game has become transformed overnight and one wonders what is in store for us in the future.

Certainly there is no doubt whatsoever that these varied fibre rods are here to stay, and also, because of the cost, wood will never return — anyway, not as we knew it. There is also absolutely no doubt that these light rods are a pleasure to fish with and whether it be children, women, men, invalids or the aged, there are rods to suit each and every one of us which can be fished with all day without tiring any of us.

At the present time rods made of these materials are costly and probably far more prone to serious breakages, as being frail and slight in appearance, they cannot stand the same abuse as rods of the past. I must admit that when I first handled these rods I was frightened to cough, let alone cast with them, they seemed so frail in my hands.

Glass-fibre rods are undoubtedly good work horses, ideal for children and beginners to learn on prior to moving on to carbon fibre when they have had some of their rough and ready habits smoothed over. I have found many of the 13 foot 6 inches to 15 foot glass-fibre rods a pleasure to fish with, especially the 14 foot rods. They are slow timers along the lines of the Greenheart range of wooden rods and can take power if need be without any undue repercussions. These rods are solid in their lift off especially in the centre piece which, to my mind, is one of the most important aspects of any rod because if a rod is soft in this field, it completely mars the cast, even a strain in the centre piece could, in the olden days entirely ruin the action of a wooden rod. I have found, however, that after continual use for several hours some glass-fibre rods can suffer from a build up of static electricity, and their casting performance deteriorates drastically from a type of fatigue, until they are lain down and rested for a while; after which time they seem to recover completely. I always use a 14 foot glass-fibre rod as my estate rod, which all and sundry can use if perchance they either have an accident with their rod or else have no suitable rod with them. This has held me in good stead for many years and is performing as well today as it ever did.

Carbon-fibre rods can be bought in practically any size or make, some whippy while others fairly stiff. All of these are again much lighter even than the glass-fibre rods as they are far slimmer than their predecessors. I, personally, do not like a whippy rod at any time because in my opinion they lack power of casting, especially in adverse conditions, as well as striking power, another point I am fanatical about. Therefore, I choose a stiffer rod in the 15–17 foot class. I find these are also relatively slow timers along the lines of the old Greenheart and have never found any difficulty in casting with them. However, I do find that they will not readily take power or forcing in the same way as wood or glass fibre, and this to my mind can be a drawback. They are excellent for switch, roll or spey casting and because of their lightness many people, ladies included, can fish with a rod of much longer length than they would have done before. This, of course, gives them far better casting ability and, more importantly, control over the fly as well as being able to overcome adverse conditions. This is a huge added benefit to a much larger range of anglers who had, in previous times, been handicapped through their inability to be able to wield rods of that length because of the physical effort involved.

Even children can start off with 10–12 foot rods with ease, at a fairly young age.

The latest advance in carbon or boron fibre rods is the hexagraph type, shaped almost like the old split cane. These may be slightly heavier, but they are undoubtedly stronger and more powerful to handle. In my opinion they are a great step forward, and can be forced without repercussions.

I must finally stress the importance of balance. No rod can serve its master to its best ability unless it has a reel and line which suit it. A rod equipped with too light a line reduces its performance to a fraction of its real ability, whilst a rod equipped with too heavy a line will be easily strained or – even worse – broken. So anglers should beware, and always read the instructions to make sure they use the line the makers recommend for each specific rod.

Even the weight of the reel is of prime importance, as too light a reel will make the rod nose heavy and this will cause needless strain on the angler's wrists; whilst too heavy a reel will add needless weight for casting, and disturbs the balance.

Reels And Equipment

There is little doubt that an angler's reel is the most important part of his equipment, because if it is not working properly he might as well pack up and go home.

I would, therefore, always advise any angler who is equipping himself out in this department not to scrimp when making this purchase. Buy the best is certainly my motto, but if you cannot afford to do so make sure that what you are buying is made by a reputable manufacturer or in other words – don't buy some cheap gimmick. This is mainly because if it jams, seizes up or some part breaks or falls off, you are left helpless unless of course you carry a spare.

I also always advise anglers to buy a wide spool reel. You can then afford to fill it with 100 yards of good quality backing and then the line of your choice. There is nothing more annoying than to find that the spool is just too small to take your new line, because then you are inclined to overfill the reel both to the detriment of the line and also risk the reel jamming or worse still, some part of the actual reel breaking.

Reels with interchangeable spools are very useful because you can then carry alternative lines ready mounted, which you can change over more or less at your will, anywhere on the river bank. However, I have always been a great fan of the old reels and in what I once called a moment of madness in the late nineteen forties, bought fifteen really high quality second-hand reels all in excellent condition, suiting both summer and spring rods, for a mere pittance. Needless to say, as it turned out, it certainly was not madness but one of the best things I have ever done as I have never had to buy a reel since. Happily I can admit that these reels are in perfect condition today and all in good working order. The secret learnt from that is to interfere with them as little as possible, except for oiling and normal maintenance. On some of the reels the bottom line guide is literally grooved with wear from the line under tension, they having been so long in use.

Anglers should always be careful as to how they reel their line back on to the reel, as many a fish is broken or lost if the line snags on the drum as the fish makes a run and this slight hesitancy can easily wrench the hook from its mouth. A sweet smooth-running reel, plenty of line and sound backing is one of the main recipes to a successful end when a fish is being played.

An angler has a choice of carrying his other equipment in a bag on his shoulders, or wearing a coat or jacket with plenty of deep pockets, maybe even both. I mainly take my tackle bag in the boot of the car and, having checked the water level and weather conditions prevailing that day, I merely take what I think I will need out of the bag and fill the pockets of my jacket or waterproof. If I find I need something else later in the day, I can easily return to the car and get it.

After all, a fly fisher is lucky in that what he requires is not nearly as bulky as that required by a bait fisher or spinner. All he needs to carry on his person, having first checked his water level and bearing in mind the time of year, is one box with a selection of flies of his favoured patterns in roughly the right size for the day, and another box filled on one side with much smaller sized flies and the other side with much larger sized flies to suit both the sublime or the ridiculous in case he might require them for shock tactics. Two old tobacco tins of tubes of varying sizes and types, including the long winged variety. An empty film container full of trebles of varying sizes and two small spools of nylon of different breaking strains. Then a bass or piece of string to help him carry his fish if he is lucky enough to catch one. I always roll the bass tight and tie a piece of string round it and then attach it by the handle to either belt or braces, as if I catch a fish I prefer to keep it in prime condition. Personally, I never carry a net, gaff or tailer as I rely on beaching my fish at all times unless I am fishing some very difficult water with extremely high banks, etc., then I would prefer a gaff, if permitted on the river I was fishing, and gaff the fish under the chin when I had played it out completely.

In this way the angler is carrying a minimal amount of gear to hinder him. If he wishes, he can carry a thermometer in his jacket handkerchief pocket and a pair of scissors round his neck on a lanyard, but in no way can he be called overloaded, even with this vast selection of gear neatly stowed away, as his entire load will be under 2 lb in weight – equally distributed. On a fine day, he can take off his jacket and leave three out of the four boxes of flies in it at the head of the pool, together with the bass. He is then left with less than ½ lb weight in his pockets.

The less one carries in the way of tackle the better because then one has more freedom to carry the fish if one is fortunate enough to catch any, and if not, at least one is not dressed up like Father Christmas, huffing and puffing between pools and sweating on the steep inclines with no hands free even to mop one's brow!

Another useful thing in which to carry tube flies are the plastic boxes with individual compartments in which Vets get their supplies delivered. These have a sliding lid and are ideal for carrying tubes in as being transparent the tube of one's choice can be quickly and easily selected. These boxes, which come in two sizes, are ultra light and fit into a deep pocket easily, while each will carry up to a dozen or more tubes.

A surgical instrument which can be of great assistance is of course surgical forceps which can be locked on to the treble or hook and because of its long reach is invaluable. Fish hooked in the back of the tongue can be quickly released without the angler getting his hands scored by its teeth. It is also a quick and easy way to remove the hook from a kelt without undue distress to the fish which can then be returned to the water virtually unharmed, whereas without it to unhook a kelt on a cold day can be frustrating and painful to the angler as well as sometimes fatal for the kelt.

Lines

In the modern era, there are so many different types of line to use one's mind almost boggles with the very thought of having to choose from the many varieties, amongst which are lead cored lines, fast, medium and slow sinkers, sunk tips and floating lines of varying types, let alone the colour range, almost as varied as the colours in a rainbow.

I must admit I only wish I could turn back the clock forty years and return to the days when the old dressed silk Kingfisher was almost the only fly line on the market in ranges from No. 1 to No. 7, in fact, a size to suit practically any rod made in those days. If you wished the equivalent of the modern floating line, you merely greased a size that suited your summer rod and kept the line for that specific purpose, or merely greased up your ordinary line when and if you wished it to float, and ungreased it when you wished to return to sunk line fishing, by running it through french chalk. I can say without doubt that in my experience these lines fitted the bill for either purpose far better than any of the best of the modern lines do today for their sole purpose. Admittedly, they needed great care and attention, but if you were willing to give them the right treatment they would serve you long and unfailing. Indeed, only last year, I had at last, loathly, to discard a No. 7 which I used for just under forty years on my 16 foot Greenheart rod, a length of service that I doubt any of the modern lines will ever have a chance of serving.

These Kingfisher lines, I would say, were on the whole medium sinkers, mainly because they were double tapered and really adequate for any mode of fishing. If you wanted to fish a deep fly you merely cast square, loosed off a yard of line, and allowed your fly to swim across the pool unaided, the exact technique used by the spinner. Medium depth was attained by casting at 60° not letting off loose line and then allowing the fly to come across unaided. Whilst shallow depths were attained by casting at 45° or 60° aided by handlining, or of course, for summer fishing, greasing the line.

Certainly today the angler can choose a specialist line for whatever he decides he wants on that day, and can carry several with him, mounted on spools which can be interchanged with the spool already on his reel, at his will. To an old hand like myself, this I think is over-simplification as I feel too much time is wasted changing from one to the other, especially if fish are down, rather like taking a bait rod, a spinning rod and a fly rod on rivers where any lure is allowed. Often in that case, the angler never gives any one lure a fair chance, as he is always thinking one of the lures on the other rods is better than the one he is using. Certainly, I fully admit that in the summer time we nearly always carried a summer rod mounted with a greased line and a stronger rod with sunk line which we used where they were best suited, and if the elements became unfavourable, such as a gale force wind getting up, we stuck to the sunk line rod for casting power.

Even today I believe a tapered medium sinker and a good floating line are really all any angler requires, provided he uses his knowledge to diversify with either if adverse or unusual circumstances prevail. With the advent of reels with interchanging spools, he is ideally equipped, and not encumbered with a lot of unnecessary baggage.

Some people however, swear by sinking tips. These admittedly, are a clever innovation of this era, and can be quickly attached to a floating line. Certainly, in order to save casting effort, they can be useful but quite frankly I do not believe that they swim a fly as neatly as either a plain floater or sinking line would do as it is really trying to compromise between the two, a thing that seldom works. I believe it fishes at more of an angle in the water than it would otherwise do. It is also more difficult to time properly in adverse conditions as with the main length of line floating and only the tip of the line sunk, it seems to lift off with a spring rather like a cork coming out of a bottle, rather than the even take off of a normal line.

Fast sinkers and lead core lines are, I suppose, adequate for use in big deep pools where snags are few and far between, such as the Tay in springtime or the Tweed in autumn. But quite frankly, I believe they are quite unnecessary, horrible to cast with and undoubtedly very hard on the rod they are cast with, unless in the hands of a very experienced angler. Other people, however, may heartily disagree.

Shooting leaded lines with only a short length of line and a reel filled with backing are impressive to watch, handled by an expert in wellnigh perfect conditions, but a nightmare to handle in really adverse conditions with high undergrowth foliage around the banks.

Whether this impressive array of lines for every possible occasion, water height, and weather condition actually helps to catch more fish, or are manufactured for the prime purpose of catching the angler himself, must be a matter of opinion.

Casts

Luckily long gone are the days of the old gut cast, the cast soakers and all which went with that era. Although when one looks back on those days, provided one followed the instructions to the letter they held us in good stead, and in all probability there were many more heavy fish landed on these than have, so far, ever been landed on nylon.

However, the fact that they were so brittle and fragile when dry and so strong and subtle when wet, was undoubtedly a worry to any angler, because during the first half an hour of the day when the long elastic pull came, one never knew whether as one tightened there would be momentary resistance on the end of the line and then the sickening ping as the cast gave, or the pleasure of an awe inspiring battle and then the reward as the fish was grassed.

Many of us cast our fly into a backwater and sat down to allow it to soak for upwards of ten minutes, on arriving at our first pool. Others meticulously took a cast soaker which was round in shape and made of aluminium fitted for the angler's pocket, with two discs of woollen blanket inside it. An hour before we ventured forth, we used to fill this narrow container with tepid water and place a 3/5 and a 5/5 Hercules cast in between the layers of wool for spring fishing, and a 8/5 and a 10/5 Hercules in it for the summer.

Then, on arrival at the river, we took our mounted cast off the rod and having replaced it with one of the soaked casts, wound it up and placed it in the soaker as a spare. We were then reasonably assured of no problems apart from if we picked up a wind knot when casting and did not notice the fact, as this was almost certainly curtains when we hooked the next fish, as few gut casts were strong enough to stand a knot.

Probably the worst time of frustration and anguish concerning casts breaking when fish were being played was the transition period between gut and nylon. I well remember an opening day at Argoed on the Welsh Dee, when my mother, father and eldest brother lost eight large fish all due to breaks when they used new American nylon casts given as a Christmas present to my father by a tenant. I can assure you that it was not safe to be on the bank of the river that day, as the annoying thing was they did not break on contact but after five to ten minutes play, and for no apparent reason. I remember about midday seeing a bundle of white cellophane packets floating past me, and knew full well these were the casts on the start of their journey back to America!!

Undoubtedly, part of the problem was that these casts copied the gut casts to the letter, and were knotted every foot or so of their length, and it was these knots which always gave. About that time I was lucky enough to be given a hank of cast called Japanese J gut, the strongest thing I have ever used – once soaked. This held me in excellent stead for spring fishing for several years afterwards, and saved me many trials and tribulations which others experienced over the transitional period, and up to the time nylon casts were properly perfected. Even to this day, however, I never trust made up nylon casts, tapered or otherwise, but always buy level spools of nylon of differing breaking strains, and if need be, make up my own taper accordingly.

In the olden days, for spring fishing we used a No. 6 or No. 7 Kingfisher, tapered line, and then a length of plaited gut some four feet in length, which we called a collar attached to the line, before finally tying the 3/5 or 5/5 gut cast leader between the collar and the heavy 6–9/° single ironed fly. The purpose of the collar was to produce a better taper from the point of the line down to the fly for both ease of casting and wind penetration and of course, this combination gave a far better lead to the heavy fly. I personally believe even to this day, that this point is of prime importance and often completely overlooked. If it is, the angler is naturally put at a severe disadvantage and handicapped accordingly, as it is completely impossible for a reasonably long length of fairly light level or tapered nylon to lead a fly that may or may not be weighted into a head wind. Often, as a result, one sees the angler's fly and point of line land in close proximity on the forward cast. If some of these anglers even used a level cast of 32 lb breaking strain in high water conditions, or a collar of three strand plaited of 20 lb, 4 feet in length, and then a leader of 25 lb, they would find a tremendous difference. Then, scale down the breaking strain of both accordingly as the season progresses, and they should find that their casting prowess is transformed especially in windy conditions, when before it was often a nightmare.

I, for my part, absolutely abhor weighted flies and would go as far as to say I despise them on the whole, but freely admit that on occasions I do use them – in what I call moments of madness, and do kill fish on them. However, I feel that quite apart from maltreating my rod, I should not need to use them, nor do I enjoy fishing with them. Because of this, I seldom use a collar but instead, a level cast of 32 lb breaking strain, 9 feet in length in high water during early spring, and

1. A 9% Gary Dog. Note the length of point in front of the barb.

2. A selection of modern tube flies.

scale down the strength of my cast thereon for the rest of the season, all according to water, weather conditions and time of season.

Again, in the summer time I have fairly strong views as to the strength of cast I use, albeit based once again on years of experience. It must be remembered, however, that I invariably use a dropper once the water temperature rises to 42°F, and this must have a slight bearing on my choice. In rocky rugged rivers, I seldom if ever go below 12 lb, but in smooth canal like waters would be prepared to go to 10 lb in low water. Below that I will not budge, except on lochs or estuaries. Both these gauges of nylon are like silk thread in comparison with the gauge of gut casts used in similar conditions in my early days, and I must admit that I do, and always will, base an awful lot of my judgement on lessons learnt in that era, whether rightly or wrongly; certainly they have held me in good stead and, therefore, I see no reason to change. It is one thing to hook a fish and another to land it, especially without the aid of an experienced ghillie who, unfortunately, is now a luxury of the past. Those who now play that role are often more like guides than personal assistants as, in their defence, they have many more rods to look after and more chores to attend to and cannot, therefore, always be in the right place at the right time.

With finer casts, there is always the chance of a quick turn of a fish chaffing the cast against a jagged sharp rock, or the quick slap of a heavy fish's tail on the taut cast, or even an unwelcome wind knot drawn too tight, or just too much strain in the excitement of the moment as the angler draws his fish to the landing place, or even wrong pressure at the wrong time by the over-excited or inexperienced. Are these risks really worth taking when they are largely unnecessary and can be avoided with forethought, and if a stronger cast that would have withstood these problems had been used. Certainly they are not, in my humble opinion.

What I think is just as important as the breaking strain of nylon is its texture. I far prefer the stiffer brands to the more pliable varieties which crinkle and kink as one ties on one's fly, and lead it, therefore, in a corkscrew fashion. The latter also fail to cut the wind and are often annoyingly blown off course at the last vital second, as well as being hopeless for use as a dropper leg because, being soft and supple, they continually foul the main leader and thereby render the dropper useless.

It is only by trial and error that an angler will find one which suits him best and he certainly has a plentiful choice if he is willing to shop around.

CHAPTER 2
FLIES

The Changing Scene of Salmon Flies

In my short lifetime it has been most interesting to see the change that has taken place in fly tying. For almost thirty years when I was a young man flies were tied immaculately to patterns that had been handed down to us from generation to generation. Admittedly during this period the odd new pattern appeared and was either named after the person who tied it, an estate or some other descriptive term. Then during the war the odd bucktail hair-winged fly appeared, so did tandem hooked flies which were really copied from and were larger editions of the old tandem sea trout fly lures.

It was not until the late 40s or the early 50s, shortly after Messrs Redpath & Co. of Inverness brought out the famed Hairy Mary fly dressing, that many professional and amateur fly dressers jumped on the band wagon and started to produce an assortment of 'bastard' patterns of hair-winged flies, many of which had the authentic bodies of the old renowned patterned flies. These were more easily tied, cheaper to produce. Many of them were very effective and some were then named. Probably the most renowned were the Stoats Tail and Silver Stoat.

Waddington then brought out his lure type waddington patterned flies, many of which were styled on the old renowned favoured pattern flies. Almost immediately afterwards the Parker Major tube flies with heavy leaded spinning-type mounts and lighter smaller tubes from the same maker heralded the arrival on the market of numerous different types of tube flies, many of which were poorly dressed and mainly tied onto a plastic body which was often too light, with no form of anchorage for the treble. This often led to the treble catching the gut above the tube during the actual cast and rendered not only the cast, but if it went unnoticed many other casts, quite useless.

Since then many modifications have greatly improved the effectiveness of the tube flies, many of which are fitted with a plastic glove that now both anchors and stabilizes the treble hook. Aluminium and brass tubes for these flies to be tied on to are fitted with a plastic liner to prevent the gut passing through the tube from becoming frayed, now give a variance of weighting to these tube flies to combat any water conditions that might prevail. Waddington flies also benefited from some of these modifications. Unfortunately over this latter era the old patterned flies, which were a work of art, are fast disappearing and it is now doubtful whether in another twenty years there will be many fly tiers left with the knowledge and experience to tie these beautiful specimens of the past. There is no doubt that labour and material costs are partly to blame for these famed old patterns being priced out of the market and any that are on the market today are generally of far poorer quality compared with the pre- and post-war specimens, with only a fraction of the minute detail and far fewer differing feathers make up the dressing of the wing.

One of the most effective modifications to tube flies was the Long Winged Variety such as the Collie and Tadpole, whereby the wing overlapped the body and hook by almost twice the latter's length. Whatever the reason is there is no doubt that its movement in the water is devastatingly attractive to fish and will move them when no other fly will.

The final innovation that has now become very popular is the long shanked treble hook which is named after the inventor Esmond Drury, many late spring and summer patterned flies are now tied on these strong shanks and they are proving to be excellent hookers of fish.

It is very interesting to compare the present flies with those of the past, both with regard to their hooking efficiency and their ability to attract fish. Also to weigh up the pros and cons of the multitude of differing lures that can now be part of an anglers' armoury. Do they really enable us to kill more fish than we used to on the old single hooked patterns? Personally I have my doubts about both these points, with admittedly certain reservations.

In the olden days for early spring fishing in high water conditions we used single ironed flies 6/$^\circ$, upwards to 10/$^\circ$. These were aptly named meathooks as some of their irons were very akin to this commodity.

There is absolutely no doubt that these were really excellent lures and would kill fish very freely, with the wide replica of differing patterned wings of all colours and varied types of bodies, we were well equipped to contend with any circumstances. The weight of fly could also be varied according to the size of iron the fly was dressed on, with the old Dee iron light and sharp in comparison with the heavy wide gap hooked varieties. The only problem was that we required heavy 15–16 foot rods of either Greenheart or steel centred split cane to not only cast them but also to drive the hook home. The latter point being of the utmost importance as from point of hook to point of barb on some irons was nearly ½ inch in length. The hook had to be literally driven home.

On many occasions I have seen the hook driven down through the fish's chin, out through the roof of its mouth or slap through the hinge and these fish seldom escaped, there rarely being any leverage with a single iron hook. It was only those that had not been struck properly that were liable to be lost.

In the modern era under the same conditions we are armed with tubes or waddingtons of every shape, size and colour as well as those of the long-tailed winged varieties. However, many of these are, in the main, sadly lacking in body variation which I personally regard as of the utmost importance and I firmly believe many of us suffer badly from this loss under certain conditions.

Our rods are on the whole much lighter but still have tremendous power and these rods, 13 foot to 17 foot 6 inches, are mostly capable of casting even the heaviest brass tube an adequate distance. Invariably, however, all but a few of us are using trebles because we fish with tubes or waddingtons, although admittedly these do not require to be driven home with the same power as the old ironed flies. I am adamant that we lose far more fish on them and I can only assume that this is due entirely to leverage on the fish's jaw by the hooks that are not embedded in its mouth. Generally this takes place when only one leg of the treble has taken a grip. Naturally when two or more legs are firmly gripped in the mouth of the fish losses are far less but strange to say this is often the exception and certainly not the rule.

In the summer time once again the angler of the past had a tremendous range of differing coloured sizes of fly with a wide variation of hackles and bodies to choose from, and varying in size from No. 10 upwards – 2/°. It is interesting to note that at this time of year most of the famed varieties had no jungle cock feathers inserted on either side of the eye of the fly, as did most of the spring patterns. There is no doubt that these represented the eyes of a fish which these cold-water patterns were meant to imitate whilst summer patterns represented plankton or waterborne invertebrates and therefore did not require eyes. All of these established patterns were dressed in every minute detail, even down to the tiniest sizes.

The irons varied tremendously in shape and size and weight but in the smaller sizes below No. 6 one had a choice of either the ordinary or long shanked hooks, both in double and single hook irons. These in my opinion were excellent hookers of fish and I always favoured the Tilson long shank hooks when available, especially for low water fishing.

At the present time during the summer months many of the old pattern single and double hooked flies are still used dressed on the old types of iron. But as well as this variety, tubes, waddingtons, and Esmond Drury flies dressed on long shanks add greatly to the choice of lure that the angler has at his command.

There is no doubt that tubes do add significantly to his repertoire as these have a different action when fished in low water conditions and cannot be simulated by flies dressed on ordinary irons. The small size, 12–16 trebles, seem to be better hookers than those used in the spring size 4–8.

Esmond Drury flies are excellent in medium and high water flows but in my opinion are too heavy for grease line fishing in low water conditions when I still prefer to fish Tilson Hook single iron flies or a small tube. Long winged flies such as Munro Killers, Tadpoles and Collies are effective in all heights of water and can be fished in grossly exaggerated sizes in comparison to the normal flies, even in the lowest water flow. When fish move to this type of fly they often take them in a most voracious manner, quite unlike their normal behaviour. It would seem, therefore, that these particular flies simulate a very favoured diet found during their sea life.

Once again flies used in the autumn are a mixture of those used in the spring and summer, all according to the weather and water conditions that prevail. As the water temperatures drop in the late autumn so the big spring flies come back into their own.

The Importance of Fly Size For Salmon

Many anglers pose the question – which is the most important factor when choosing a fly, the size of the fly or the pattern? I think most experienced anglers would agree that in nearly every case the answer is the size is of more importance. Certainly at the start of the day when an angler has no prior knowledge, as salmon have the most unpredictable taking habits, as to whether his quarry is going to take freely, be choosey, or remain down and stiff to move on that particular day.

The angler is, therefore, best to err on the safe side and choose a fly slightly on the small size of what his experience tells him for the first fishing of the pool. If the fish are keen they will take it, and if they don't the angler can then change up in size, and fish the pool again having not harmed his chances in any way. If, however, the angler selects a fly larger than is required on that day, the risk he takes is that the fish will fluff or splash at it, instead of taking properly, and the chances that the fish will then be pricked in the process and not rise again to the fly are extremely high. The angler can, therefore, easily lose two or three chances that he otherwise might well have capitalised on, through this slight error of judgement.

Another question I am often asked is, how much can an angler err by before the risk of spoiling his chances? This is, of course, a far more difficult question, which really depends largely on the time of year and also, more importantly, on the water temperature as well as river flow. In the early springtime in cold water temperature and high river flows, I doubt whether ½ inch in size would really make any material difference for the first fishing of a pool, but in lower water conditions at the same time of year, and warmer water temperature, I would advise being no more than ¼ inch.

In late April and May, when temperatures are considerably higher, and also later in the year when optimum temperatures are more like the norm, the angler has to be far more accurate and then an error of one size in size of fly can be sufficient to cause damage resulting in pulls from fish, rather than solid takes.

There is absolutely no question of doubt in my mind that during the summer months even the most experienced of us err on the large side, and often make the mistake of believing that high water levels at that time of year require larger flies. This, however, does not always follow.

I well remember motoring up to fish the Helmsdale one day late in May and on arriving at my beat, I found the river running fairly high. The ghillie came over to my car and looked at the flies I had mounted on my rod, which were a No. 9 Hairy Mary on the dropper, and a No. 6 Stoats Tail in the tail fly position. He immediately said my tail fly was far too big, and produced out of his box a miniscule blue and black tube, barely ¼ inch in length. As I watched astounded, he changed my fly for his and led me down to the first pool. In no time at all I rose a fish, and the very next cast caught it on the tiny tube fly, a nice 10 lb fish, slightly stale as it had been up a while.

That was only the beginning. To cut a long story short, we had seven fish between us, as I was sharing my rod with a friend, six of these fell to the blue and black tube and one to the Hairy Mary, which looked twice the size of the very lightly dressed slim-lined tube. Quite frankly, anybody would have been quite warranted in fishing as large a fly as a No. 1 on that particular day according to water flow, and peat stain in the river, as well as it being a dull day with a strong west wind.

In the early springtime I think anglers can often err the other way by using a 2 inch weighted fly instead of a much larger fly mounted on an aluminium tube. At that time of year I often use a long-tailed tube, 6–9 inches overall, and fish it fast. On many occasions in January, I have brought fish up to these flies literally head and tailing onto them on the surface, just like they would when taking a tiny fly fished on a greased line in June. On one of the deepest pools we have on the Cassley, the Round pool, over 70 per cent of the fish we catch break the surface as they take the fly in January, February, March and April, and I would far prefer to bring fish up to the surface to take my fly, rather than put a heavy weighted fly down to them.

Once you have fished the first four holding pools on the beat, you will know by then whether the fish are in a taking mood, or whether they are going to be stiff and down. If they are taking freely, keep on with the flies you are using. If not, you should begin to think of shock tactics to wake them up. The first obvious change is, if you have been fishing medium heavy flies deep revert to much larger lighter flies, and fish these faster and vice versa. If this change fails to work, first fish a much smaller ordinary patterned fly, and then if this fails, put on the biggest fly in your box and go down to the tail of the best holding pool on the beat, and back it up quietly casting fairly square. This often does the trick and moves fish which sometimes take, whilst other times they will rise or swirl to it, and never touch the fly. When they do this, immediately change back to your original choice at the start of the day and you will often find that having been woken up out of their lethargy by the abnormal fly, they will then take the normal one.

I well remember a very famed angler telling me in my youth that you should first fish a pool with the fly of your choice, then the sublime followed by the ridiculous, and only then had you given the fish in it a fair chance to take. Wise words of wisdom which have held me in good stead on numerous occasions.

Finally, a fairly recent innovation to fly types, the long-winged variety with a sweeping wing of black Collie dog hair overlapping the length of the body of the tube or iron by one and a half times. The most common of these, the Collie Dog or Tadpole, are famed for their catching ability throughout a large part of Scotland. These are particularly efficient in the spring, as well as throughout the entire season. These flies can be tied from 9 inches long down to ¼–¾ inch and can be used in any height of water, or season of the year. The most useful sizes are probably dressed on 1–1½ inches and 2 inch aluminium tubes, and these are used when 1 inch, 2 inch and 3 inch ordinary tubes are bing fished in the spring.

The smaller varieties of ¼–½ inch and ¾ inch are used really as normal flies, such as the Munro Killer, but I have on many, many occasions killed salmon with 1–1½ inch Collies, 2½–3½ inches in overall length in the lowest of low water conditions when No. 8 or No. 9 patterned flies were the norm. The very large Collies are excellent to use as shock tactics at the end of a dour day, when, if used to back up a good holding pool and fished fairly fast, they can be quite effective either to catch fish or at least to move them.

Seemingly with these flies, the long overlapping tail appears to be discounted regarding length by the fish, as an ordinary fly of similar length fished under similar circumstances would, I am quite certain, be completely disregarded. It is also interesting to note that salmon nearly always take these flies by their head and rarely, if ever, by the tail below the trebles, they do, however, often take these flies head on upstream. Whatever it is about these long-winged flies, they are fatally attracted to them and often take them viciously, quite unlike the normal take, sometimes breaking water with the fly actually in the mouth whilst other times the pool just erupts where the fly is, and other times the rod is nearly pulled out of the angler's hand.

Flies, Over or Under Dressed

This is really a question of the angler's own preference, but I must admit from my own experience of over fifty years as a salmon fisherman, I have found both very effective on their particular day.

What I do believe is of far more importance is that the body is never more than lightly veiled so that its tinsel or ribbing is given the entire freedom to radiate light as the fly is buffeted in the current flow and varied underwater and surface eddies. This I deem to be one of the most essential parts of fly fishing for salmon, because it is this glint or flicker that alerts a salmon of the fly's presence, just the same as a light flickering on a hillside at night would immediately catch our eye and then our attention too. This is particularly important when the water is either peaty or turbid late on in the year, when a tiny fly can pass time and time over many fish lying in a pool and, because of its insignificance, goes on unnoticed until at last a glint from the tinsel alerts fish of its presence. Having been alerted, they often become inquisitive enough to take notice and then, eventually, to take the fly.

Nearly all the immaculately tied, patterned flies of the past carried either silver or gold tinsel on the body, and also jungle cock feathers in the form of an eye on either side of the eye of the fly, which also radiated light. Seldom, if ever, were these features masked except by a thin hackle or tiny body feather. When the first tubes came out they were often tied more like a bottle brush than a fly which would have masked any body ever made, as the hair wing completely encircled the tube. They looked like nothing on earth, but did kill fish all the same.

Now fly tiers have become more conscious of their misdemeanours in the past, and dress the tubes with a main top wing, and the aluminium or brass tube is exposed. Some are being tied with their own body dressed on top of the aluminium or brass bodies which the tubes are made of. Few tubes are now made with the original plastic bodies, except in the smaller sizes.

At the same time as the tube fly became so popular, a Waddington type fly with an eye with a wire body connected to a treble hook stabilized to an eye at the tail of the body was also produced. These were dressed with the old standard bodies of the famed authentic patterns with a thin veil of feather plumes like a light long hackle, surrounding much of the fly. These on the whole were a far more

44

realistic way of copying the older masters than the first large tubes which were produced.

The first small tubes were mainly tied on short plastic tubes, dressed to patterns such as the Hairy Mary, Stoats Tail, Thunder and Blue Charm. The former two were heavily dressed, whilst the latter lightly. All were reasonably effective, with probably the Hairy Mary and Stoats Tail most favoured.

Heavy Parker type tubes were dressed on a light metal tube, wide enough to allow a weighted spinning mount to be passed through the tube with a red bead halfway down the mount. This was to prevent the mount being pulled too far through the body of the tube when the tube was fishing, and prevented the hooks being masked by the tube. Most favoured patterns in this type of fly were the Garry Dog, Hairy Mary, Shrimp and Akroyd. These could also be good if a weighted fly was required, and were easier to cast than the plain brass tubes.

When one looks back on the past to the old 1–9/° patterned flies used mainly for spring fishing in those days few, if any, were not fully dressed when bought new, and all were very effective. Only when they were well worn after being fished with for years did they really become threadbare, and many of these old favourites still did the trick even then with hardly a feather left on the wing. I still have a 10/° Silver Grey with barely an inch long tuft of wing left, but the body hardly worn at all. Even today I use it if I am stuck, and so far have caught 103 fish on it.

In the olden days, for summer patterns some were very lightly dressed whereas others such as the Lady Caroline, were fairly drab and heavily dressed. It is my firm opinion that this fly, and others similar, were dressed specifically for greased line fishing to simulate plankton, a vegetation merely hanging inert in the current in suspension.

If one looks at the famed bob flies used for boat fishing on West Coast lochs, either for salmon or sea trout, and for that matter brown trout. The Black Penal were originally very sparsely dressed with a very fine hackle veiling the body, whilst another popular one, the Loch Ordie was dressed more like a bottle brush to serve the same purpose, both can be equally effective on either a calm or rough day.

Certainly today the modern fly dresser still dresses a mixture of heavy and lightly dressed flies and their wings on the whole are more sparsely tied, many of them now with hair rather than feathers.

However, the rage now seems to be to tie many patterns on the Esmond Drury treble hook shank. These, except in the smaller sizes, in my humble opinion, appear to be both heavy and clumsy with a wide body necessitated, mainly due to the heavy shank. However, no doubt some people are satisfied with them or they would not buy them.

In low water flows I have, and always will, as first choice, favour the lightly dressed flies, but am far too long in the tooth to disregard completely the heavier dressed ones, and will always carry them. These I will definitely try before I am beat, as I am a great believer in trial and error, and sometimes a change from the lightly dressed to the heavily dressed does the trick. Salmon are fickle in their ways and it always pays to try everything rather than stick to what you favour. Often it is the complete opposite which does the trick in the end. Very often these very ugly heavily dressed types of fly swim at a depth which suits these unpredictable creatures on that day, as they can be far more buoyant than their slim-lined counterparts. Depth at which your fly fishes can be a most important factor on many occasions and along with presentation, fly size, type and speed at which the fly travels, all are well worth varying when fish are stiff. Even such a small alteration to any one of these can make all the difference.

Salmon: What They Will Take

One of my earliest recollections from my youth was being out for a walk on a Sunday with a great old fishing friend of my father's on the bank of the Upper Cassley in early August. It was a very hot day and Sandy Prentice, who was then in his late seventies, decided to rest for a while, so he sat down on a knoll beside the river where a fast rapid run entered a still dark pool.

Several salmon kept leaping in the main body of the pool, but after a while our attention was drawn to a salmon which kept head and tailing very quietly, just where the run entered the pool. We both soon noticed that this fish was rising to and taking a type of heather moth, which were hatching on nearby marshy ground beside the river, and being blown by the wind on to the surface of the water and floating down into the pool.

We watched fascinated as this fish devoured these moths in numerous numbers, literally sucking them quietly off the surface. Shortly afterwards the hatch of these moths almost ceased, and the fish then only rose very occasionally, but still in the same manner.

Old Prentice turned to me and suggested that I should search around in the rushes and heather to see if I could find any similar insects, and if I did, to place them on the fast current so that they would be swept over the fish in order to see if they would also be taken.

The first insects I came across were two daddy long-legs and a grasshopper, all of which I carefully carried to the side of the river and placed one by one, at about two minute intervals, on the surface of the water. As each daddy long-leg floated over him, the salmon rose quietly and sucked them off the surface, but when the grasshopper floated over him he made a great dive at it and took it leaving a swirl on top of the water.

For nearly half an hour I searched for insects and plied to and fro the river bank, releasing them on the surface. Nearly every time an insect floated over him, he sucked it in quietly, but whenever a grasshopper was released he made a far more vicious rush at it.

Sandy Prentice was delighted at this performance and rubbing his hands in glee at the thought of how many fish he was going to catch on the Monday, as he knew he would be fishing there next morning.

Needless to say, when he returned there next day, there was no sign of the hungry salmon nor did it appear when Sandy plied the surface of the water with numerous insects of every shape and size.

I must also admit that this was the first and last time I witnessed a salmon rising continuously for almost an hour freely taking surface insects, but I have often seen salmon take the occasional fly off the surface of a river, and also a loch. But there is little doubt that a drowning fly or other insect is much favoured by salmon, hence the effectiveness of the dibbled, dapped, trailed flies, or the fly fished on the riffling hitch method, and even the dry fly but few anglers persevere with this latter method in this country for some unknown reason, in spite of its effectiveness in North America. However, at long last a book has been written by Knowles, describing his experiences in fishing a Yellow Dolly dry fly.

During my long experience of fly fishing for salmon and endless hours spent on the banks of many rivers, I have witnessed salmon taking unusual objects on several occasions. The first time was on the Welsh Dee, when I watched a very large salmon rise and take, and then eject, several leaves in a space of half an hour in the still deep water near the tail of the Major Pool. Although I tried to simulate this, by attaching a leaf to my hook, I failed to prevent it dragging on the surface, and my efforts failed miserably.

Another point of interest on the same river shortly after the war resulted from a certain tackle maker painting his spiral weights red in colour. Both when spinning and prawn fishing when I used these weights I got several heavy pulls from fish, and on winding in found the salmon's teeth marks clearly imprinted on the lead, which had been readily taken in preference to the bait. Needless to say, these coloured weights were quickly rejected.

I remember an occasion in the Gorge above the falls on the Cassley in the late fifties, when Willie Mackay (my late keeper) and I were cutting scrub bushes to open up a new pool. As Willie was chopping down a sapling alder with a small hatchet, chippings from his axe fell onto the surface of the water and not one but two salmon rose to and took these chippings, on several occasions. In this case it was interesting to note that whereas one fish ejected the chipping immediately he had closed his mouth on it, the other fish took the chipping down with him as he returned to his lie, and only released it several moments later. As we did not have a rod with us, we could not try and catch these fish.

Finally, one day when conditions seemed ideal on the Shin, I fished the falls beat diligently several times without a move, and just before I was due to pack up as it was nearly six o'clock, Willie Macdonald and

I were sitting on the rocks beside the steep path at the shoulder of Cromarty, whiling away time as we selected another fly for the final fishing of the pool. Having tied the fly on, I idly flicked the stub of my cigarette onto the surface of the pool as I got up to fish. Both to my amazement and annoyance, a good fish, over 12 lb in weight, swam sedately up to the cigarette butt and having taken it, disappeared back into the deep. If there was ever a case of adding insult to injury, that was a prime example.

Unusual Flies

When I lived on the Welsh Dee, one of our most favoured patterns during the spring fishing season was a Silver Wilkinson. I well remember one particular fly in my father's collection, a 1/° size Silver Wilkinson which he had used for years. It had become so battered after killing numerous fish that its entire wing had disappeared, and all that was left of the fly's dressing was a wizened throat hackle, the silver body and yellow tippet. Even so, my father and his old Welsh ghillie, Robert Jones, had tremendous faith in this particular fly and used it regularly in preference to all others when they fished the Pentre Pool from a coracle in medium water heights, and time and time again it proved to be successful.

I remember one Saturday in mid-April in 1939, one of the best seasons on the Welsh Dee, when we went up to the Pentre Pool. My father and Robert were in the coracle, and I was watching from the bank. Having fished the pool and drawn a blank with a Mar Lodge, as Robert walked back to the head of the pool carrying the coracle on his back, my father sat on the bank whilst he changed his fly. As he looked in his fly box for his favourite fly, he discovered he had taken the wrong fly box and had left the other at home. However, undeterred, he selected a fairly new 1/° Silver Wilkinson and tied it on his cast. Once again they fished the pool diligently from top to bottom without moving a fish, although several fish jumped as they fished the pool down. Robert insisted that they should fish the pool once more, and my father this time selected a Yellow Torrish of the same size. Having seen them launched at the head of the pool I decided, being young and keen at the time, to run home and fetch my father's fly box which contained his lucky fly, in spite of the fact that the house was some mile away and all up hill. So without saying a word I left the scene quietly and having made sure I had the right fly box this time and that his favoured fly was in it, I returned to Pentre Pool. When I got there, I saw two disconsolate fishermen finishing off the last few yards of the pool, still without so much as a move from a fish.

As they landed, I produced the fly box from my pocket, and suggested they try the old favourite fly. I firmly believe that neither had any will to try the pool down for a fourth time, but seeing that I had gone home for the fly, neither wished to offend me.

Sure enough, almost as soon as my father had started fishing with his favoured fly, he rose a fish but the fish would not come again, so they passed on down the pool. Then, halfway down the pool, he caught a beauty of 23 lb and then at the tail a 19 lb.

Highly satisfied, I left them to try a cast myself lower down the beat in the Summer House Pool, where I was shortly joined by my mother.

We fished on till nearly six o'clock, during which time my mother caught a 17½ lb but I was blank, and as we walked home up the steps there was still no sign of my father and Robert. When eventually they did come home, they had no less than seven fish, three of them over 20 lb, and all caught on the threadbare Silver Wilkinson.

Was it confidence in the fly or something that the fish wanted on that particular day which was the key to my father's success? Luckily we will never know, but I saw that fly catch fish when nothing else would so often that I am quite certain it was not a fluke. I also remember many times stripping down Silver Wilkinsons to simulate this particular fly, but although I caught fish on them, they never lived up to the reputation of the old favourite.

Another time I was with an old ghillie who honestly believed that the masterful skill of fly tiers was just an expensive luxury. All he used was an ordinary 4–9/° iron with its body either painted silver, red or a mixture of these colours in the spring, and gold or orange in the summer and autumn on No. 8 – 1/° shanks. For a wing he used strips of neckerchiefs or coloured handkerchiefs tied to the eye of the hook, generally two or three strips per fly. These horrific looking flies, I must admit, did kill fish in numbers, often right behind people fishing with beautifully dressed patterned flies, as old Tom was always told by his employer to fish down behind his guests.

Tom's cousin, Murdo, was another person with firm beliefs. He worked for another estate who were supplied with flies by one of the best fly tiers I ever bought flies from. Murdo believed in having only five patterns – Mar Lodge, Silver Grey, Green Highlander, Jock Scott and Black Dr, in all the known sizes from No. 9 up to 9/°. Once the water temperature rose to over 50°F. Murdo used to pull the jungle cock and gawdy feathers out of his well used flies in the smaller sizes, so that he was left with very drab coloured flies without jungle cock to imitate plankton or waterborne invertebrates, rather than go to the expense of purchasing other patterns such as Lady Caroline, Blue Charm, etc., which were more renowned for these purposes.

I also remember another ghillie who insisted on tying flies with very thick bodies, at least twice the width of a normal fly's body. Certainly he killed just as many fish as anyone else. He once gave me one dressed in the pattern of a Dee Butcher, on a size 1 iron. I remember having remarkable success on this fly if I used it in low water, when one would normally have been fishing a No. 8 or 9. It was particularly effective in deep pools, just at the tail of the stream entering the pool, where the current was becoming slack. Seemingly, this thick woollen body made the fly more buoyant, and the fly used to come up very close to the surface. Time and time again, I moved fish with this fly when all else had failed. One could see the fly clearly, just under the surface, and the fish used to come at it at high speed and generally take very solidly.

In the modern era, more and more fly tiers are beginning to use flexy, luminous, man-made tinsel type material, mixed in with the hair or feathered wing of the fly, or as the hackle. This material not only scintillates light, but also movement, and seems very effective as both these actions help to draw the fish's attention to the fly and certainly tend to alert fish of its presence, a task which was previously left in the hands of the silver or gold tinsel body, which had more or less the same effect by glinting as the fly gyrated in the buffeting currents. There is no doubt some of these modern flies, tied in this manner, are very effective.

The Long Winged Variety

It has always fascinated me as to why flies dressed on a No. 1 iron with an appreciably longer wing overlapping the hook are often so much more effective in comparison with the more commonly dressed flies whereby the wing of the fly and hook iron are the same length.

I first came across these Long Winged Varieties in the late 1930s on the Welsh Dee, when my father owned the Argoed water. He had a great friend, a doctor at Chirk, who regularly fished at Argoed in his spare time. Being an ardent fly fisherman Dr Hampson used to tie flies during the long winter evenings and one of the patterns he favoured most was one of these Long Winged Varieties, which he gave the descriptive name of the 'Yellow Long Tail'. This fly was dressed on a No. 1 iron with silver tinsel body and yellow throat hackle. Its wing consisted of two long feathers dyed yellow, and one dyed maroon, these feathers overlapped the iron of the fly by approximately two inches. In those days at Argoed the tendency, particularly in the early part of the season, was to favour yellow coloured flies with the Yellow Torrish, Yellow Peril and Bullfinch being amongst the most popular patterns.

I well remember on many, many occasions when either my father, a fly purist, or his friend were finding fish difficult to come by they would immediately resort to the Yellow Long Tail, very often with the resultant success that they were hoping for. It was also very effective in dead low water conditions in spite of its length, and would kill fish freely under conditions when size 8 or 10 flies were the norm for those particular water heights or that season of the year. It was also excellent for luring a fish which had risen to a previous fly, into making a mistake and seldom failed in this respect, unless of course the fish had been pricked when he moved to the first fly.

After that, during the war, several patterns of flies with tandem double hooks joined by plaited gut came on the market, and these were quite effective. However, having become an ardent supporter of the 'Yellow Long Tail' over the intervening years, I merely cut the gut joining the second flight of hooks and fished these varieties as Long Winged flies, to my mind to even greater effect, as they added several new patterns to my armoury of this type of fly.

During my spell in the forces, I was posted to Aldergrove, in Northern Ireland, and during my stay there, because of my intense love of fishing I used to spend a lot of my spare time browsing round tackle shops comparing the Irish patterned flies to those I knew so well both on the Welsh Dee and also on the Kyle of Sutherland rivers in Scotland. One day I noticed an unusual pattern of the Long Winged type, dressed on a size 8 iron. It had a vivid dark jade wing, hot orange hackle and white silk body, out of interest I bought two of these and sent them home to my father. In spite of the fact that it was July when I sent them to him, not one of the most productive months at Argoed, he had really remarkable success on them at a time when no fish had been killed for several weeks on the fly. Unfortunately, after I had left Ireland these specimens were misplaced and I never found them again. I tried hard to find a new source of supply but without a pattern to copy I was not successful.

During the last decade, this Long Winged Variety of fly has become very, very popular in the north of Scotland and flies such as the Collie Dog and Tadpole are now amongst the most productive, and popular patterns are to be found and used in differing sizes from 9 inch in length to ½ inch throughout the entire season of the year. The Blue Elver, another feather-winged variety has also proved itself but probably more so on the west coast rivers than those on the east side of the county.

The Collie was originally produced with just a long tuft of black hair wing tied onto a black No. 1 size hook; it had no body or hackle but was very effective even so. It appears not to matter as to whether the long overlapping wing consists of feathers, hair or a combination of both. Nor does it matter whether it is dressed on large or small tubes or single or double hook irons, however, if dressed on a tube it is better only to have a top plume of hair and imperative that the hair is not dressed around the entire circumference of the tube.

I can only imagine that the secret of these Long Winged Varieties of flies lies in the unsupported over-lap of the wing being given far more freedom of movement than the normally dressed flies. This allows it freedom to quiver, tremor and wag as it is pulled against the current. Without doubt these varieties fish much better if they are moved quickly through the water by quick hand-line action. They are also really ideal for backing up a pool and very large sizes often prove successful when used as shock tactics at the end of a blank day. On numerous occasions, by using these tactics an hour or two before packing in for the day, I have not only saved the blank, but also turned the day into a most productive outing.

It is extremely probable that these flies resemble an elver or other long-tailed variety of fish found on the feeding grounds at sea, and obviously a favoured diet. When taking these patterns, and particularly so when using the Collie Dog pattern, the salmon seem to behave in a most ferocious manner and literally attack these lures fiercely. Certainly quite different from their normal behaviour when taking an ordinary fly. I have often seen them jump on top of the fly, in which case the pool explodes as they take, whilst at other times they come out of the water with the fly actually in their mouths. Sometimes these ferocious tactics lead to them missing the fly altogether, but often they will come again to the fly when it is re-presented to them, usually with more success.

Why these very long flies are so effective in dead low water is, however, a bit more of a mystery as flies of these patterns, of 2–4 inches in length, readily take fish under these conditions when the normal fly size would be a size 8–10. I can only imagine that these flies must imitate some delicacy, in resemblance to these patterns, to be found in the warmer gulf stream currents along with different species of tiny fish.

CHAPTER 3

CONTROL OF THE FLY

Rod Tip Control

This is amongst the most important aspects of angling, mainly because there is little point in being able to cast a long line if, once the fly lands on the water, the angler is not able to keep in contact with and, to a certain degree, keep control over his fly as it fishes out the cast.

With the rod tip the angler has the means, if he so wishes, of controlling the speed that his fly fishes out his cast, provided the angler is willing to use it. He can simply, by adjusting the angle of his rod, viz a viz the current flow, either slow down or quicken up the speed the fly traverses across the width of the pool, or on occasions allow his fly to pause or hesitate over likely places for brief moments. He can also lead his fly close into the bank in order to search various nooks and crannies there.

If the angler does not choose to take advantage of this means of control and merely follows the angle of his line with his rod tip, he is then leaving the control of his fly entirely in the hands of the current and eddies of the pool, and thereby often loses control over both the speed and depth at which the fly crosses the width of the pool, and for this reason is often completely out of contact with it when a fish takes. In other words he chucks and chances it, and admittedly sometimes it works. However, the angler who gives considerable thought to the finer points of casting and control has a far better chance of improving his rate of success.

Unless an angler knows the water he is fishing intimately through long experience, or has a helpful ghillie to guide him, he really has no accurate knowledge of where the best lies are in each pool he comes to, or where in the width of the pool fish will be. He has, therefore, really got to cover as much of his water as his ability allows him and hope for the best.

He is best, therefore, to start at the head of the pool with just the length of line he has on the rod and cast out square to the current, and work this short line literally with his rod tip square to the current, and moving it ever so slightly upstream until his fly has fished out this narrow arc. The angler then lengthens a yard, cast by cast, until he has lengthened out his line sufficiently to cover the full width of the pool, or in the case of a wide pool the length of line he intends to fish the rest of the pool out with. By fanning out his fly with this method, he is ensuring that he does not miss any fish that may be lying close to him at the neck of the pool, fish that can so easily be missed by the angler who stands at the head of the pool and simply lengthens out line so that his fly has reached the far side of the pool before he bothers to fish out his first cast. By controlling these short casts on his rod tip until his line is as long as his rod can control in comfort without the aid of handlining, the angler saves himself the need to false cast. Once this length of line is attained, then he must begin to handline at the end of each cast to enable him to cast a longer line. Even when I have reached this length of line, I still believe in keeping control of my fly with the square rod tip, always working it quietly upstream as I handline at the same time. This not only ensures that the fly is always buoyant and kept free from snagging, but also allows me to be in complete contact with it. Only if and when I need to lead it close into the side of the bank I am fishing from do I lead it there with my rod tip, and compensate for this downstream rod movement by hand-lining much faster as I do so. Once my fly has been led in close to my side of the river, I immediately square my rod tip again to lead it back out towards the centre of the river. This reduces the risk of the salmon taking directly downstream of the rod tip, which seldom leads to success and at the same time brings the rod into a useful casting position for the next cast.

In very wide pools where the angler has no hope of casting across the entire width of the river, he must remember that there is every likelihood of his fly landing on the water in the very close proximity of where fish are lying. It, therefore, improves an angler's chance of catching one of these fish if he can get his fly to hesitate for a brief moment before starting its traverse across the pool, to enable fish to size it up before it flashes past them. I personally believe in casting at 60° across river, rather than 45° and, as usual, square my rod across current. Both these movements I find adequately suit this purpose.

However, some people prefer to mend their line immediately the fly lands, this also serves the purpose but, in my opinion, the line is then aligned too parallel to the current flow and does not lead the fly as smoothly once it begins to move across river.

If there is an obvious swirl on the surface of the pool, which usually denotes an underwater lie or a lull between two streams close to my side of the river, I believe in allowing my fly to sweep through these likely places, then quietly move my rod back to the square position to the current, in order to take my fly back through them again, moving it out towards the centre of the river, then allow it to pause over the lie before finally sweeping it through the lie again as it continues on its journey to my bank. In places like that, I would probably allow my

Fishing a quiet glide

Using the square rod tip to control the fly

first cast over this spot to continue on its journey through the lie, then cast over the lie twice more in the manner described above.

For all these varied manoeuvres so far described, I keep my rod tip low about 3 feet above water level, and before recasting raise it first to the high rod tip position, in order to make sure my line and fly are buoyant as I handline at the same time and then lift off for the recast. By adopting this procedure, you are easing the burden on your rod and significantly reducing any chance of your fly snagging just before lift off, and get a far cleaner and smoother lift off into the bargain, which is the very essence of good timing.

Rod tip control with a high rod tip is in general more related to the dibbled dropper or trailed tail fly, both of which can be very deadly methods of fishing during much of the summer or early autumn months. Both these methods of fishing can only be fished on a relatively short line, but a long rod is definitely a big advantage as the added height above water level improves the control of the surface fly, and helps keep the line clear of the current.

When using these methods, finger tip control is essential to keep the dibbled fly teetering on the broken surface, or drag the bigger tail fly on the surface. A combination of lowering or raising the rod as the fly traverses the width of the river keeps the fly in even motion, holding it on either side of the current and in other crucial swirls and boils which denote likely lies, sometimes moving it quickly away to tempt fish to grab it as it seemingly tries to escape. In windy, gusty conditions the art of rod tip control can be very sorely tested as it is infuriating to see the dibbled fly blown off the surface just as a fish comes to it, and can be just as frustrating as trying to control the dap for sea trout under the same conditions.

One of the main things to watch out for when using these methods is useful stances on the bank that can not only get the angler closer to the bank, but due to their height, enable the angler to use a longer line in order to cover more water. The experienced dibbler will soon learn to recognise those which help him to gain more control over his flies.

Handline Movement

Many people regard handlining as merely a necessity in order to help the rod one is using to throw a longer line than the rod is capable of doing without being aided. In other words, having drawn in line prior to casting, this line is released on the forward cast and then, if the cast is timed right, this loose line is carried out by the impetus of the line that is cast by the rod, or shooting the line. These people handline usually at the end of the cast, just when the fly has completed its traverse of the pool.

Others believe in handlining from the very start of the cast, and I am certainly a firm believer in this school of thought. In fact, as soon as my fly lands on the water, I immediately pull in two 18 inch draws to ensure I am in absolute contact with my fly before it begins to traverse across the width of the pool, and then according to the amount of current flowing through the pool I draw in my line as I handline quietly the whole time my fly is fishing in the pool. If there is fast current, I will probably only draw in about 2 inches per draw, just sufficient to allow me to be in absolute contact with it. If, however, the pool is a fairly quiet one, then I will draw in as much as 18 inches to 2 feet. By drawing in line over your index finger, you are able to detect the slightest tremor or touch, no matter how light it is, and will be able to distinguish between a buffet from the current and the move from a fish, even a touch as light as a leaf can easily be detected.

Over and above this type of handlining motion for contact, I believe in simulating the movement of what I am trying to imitate with my fly on that particular day. When I am trying to imitate a small fish, I try and transmit the obvious swimming motion into my fly, entirely by handline control, often speeding up the movement or else slowing down the movement, in order to tempt my quarry.

Especially when I try shock tactics by using a ridiculous sized fly, I speed up my handlining control and fish these extremely quickly through the water, and often back up at the same time to make my quarry believe that my fly is trying to escape from it. When I try to imitate water-borne invertebrates, I then handline in very short draws in uneven bursts. Plankton, which is a vegetation, must have no movement but instead be allowed to hang inert high in the water. Therefore, on this occasion it is the only time I never handline at all.

*3. A selection of large patterned Spring flies, and (below) 5 – 6%
patterned flies.*

The neck of the Round Pool with the cupped stone on the far bank

If I am using long-winged flies I adopt a long flowing fast motion, especially when fishing the larger sizes.

All in all, I am a great believer in altering my speed of presentation rather than keeping to the same monotonous delivery throughout the entire fishing period, and I am quite certain this pays off. When I fish with a partner, or behind another angler, I watch my companion carefully to ascertain what form of presentation he is adopting, and having made myself aware of his angle of cast, speed of retrieve, etc., I adopt an entirely different form.

In long narrow guts between rocky outcrops, or narrow runs, I seldom bother to cast but instead lengthen my line by simply letting out line and controlling my lure entirely with rod tip control and handline motion. Virtually allowing the fly to harl the pool from side to side of its width, guided by the rod tip, whilst I quicken or slow down its action by handline control.

When I am dibbling or trying to fluff my tail fly on the surface of the water, although this is largely controlled by rod tip motion, in order to extend the length beyond what you can control with the rod tip, you have to do this by handlining sometimes letting out line and other times drawing in quickly to stop the fly from submerging.

The same applies to controlling your bob fly so that it bounces on top of the waves when you are fishing from a boat for salmon or trout, and particularly applies to dapping especially when the wind is gusty or flukey, and not steady. In the latter case, finger tip control to allow the fly to flit across the waves and prevent it from drowning requires quick and definite handline action, and rod tip control.

A question often asked is, what do you do with the line that you have drawn in? Should you coil it in your hand neatly, or merely throw it down in front of you? Certainly the former looks far neater and in theory should be the most efficient, but in practice I have always found the latter serves the purpose adequately and adopt this course. Far too often I have seen the angler who coils his line in his hand get into serious trouble when he hooks a wild fish with the coiled line shooting up, when released, as the fish makes a long run, and then jamming in the lowest ring of the rod often with disastrous consequences. Whereas in the same predicament, the loose line often lying floating on the water, runs out smoothly with no ill effect. Only in situations where there are ill-kempt banks would I contemplate favouring the coiled method.

67

Short Line Fishing Technique

This method of fishing is not commonly used in the modern era, but when I was a boy many of the old Highland ghillies were past masters at this art. Naturally it is best suited to narrow runs or deep small pools often associated with rivers to be found either on the West Coast or Northern areas of Scotland, where these narrow rivers often descend steeply seawards, through rocky rugged ravines or gorges, where this type of fishing can be used to great effect. This method, however, can also be effective on the big pools of much larger rivers, if fished from the bank alongside which the deep water lies.

The object of fishing with a short line is to have as little line on the water as possible, so that the fly is under the complete control of rod tip movement and, therefore, can be slowed down or quickened up at the will of the angler, and also if need be hung over a particular lie for a moment or two. This controlled type of presentation has a definite advantage over the normal presentation on a long or medium length of line when a considerable amount of line lies on the surface of the water and is therefore, particularly when a floating line is being used, largely in the hands of surface currents and eddies. Because these currents and eddies catch the floating line and kink and twist it irregularly as the line passes over them, causing the fly at the end of the cast to follow the path of the line like a puppet on the end of a string, as it snakes and twists from buffet to buffet, often crazily and completely outwith the angler's control.

I well remember two old ghillies, Sandy and Angus Ross, who had been on the Cassley for years before my father bought Rosehall, and were with him until they retired in the early 1940s. The old men fished with 16–18 foot rods, and when fishing the Cemetery pool and the rocky pools above it, rarely if ever, had more than their cast in the water. Both believed in flicking their fly out square across the current and bringing it back towards them in little jerky actions, whilst in the narrow gorges they cast downstream across the current, and kept waggling their rod tip up and down very quickly to inject movement into their fly. Both these old men could move fish regularly after their guests had completely failed to get a move.

My father studied this method of fishing carefully, and could move and catch fish in the Cemetery pool right up to his ninetieth year in 1970, and undoubtedly killed more fish in that pool than anyone else I have ever seen fish it, but whereas Sandy and Angus had always favoured the tail of the pool or the Cemetery gorge, my father preferred what we call the hacking block, a lie where two streams meet off the point of the shingle.

All three of these men fished these pools very akin to the manner a boat angler would fish for trout, albeit that they only used a single fly but they did persevere, altering their angle of cast and speed of retrieve with rod tip control. When they moved a fish it would either take solidly underwater, or make a dimple or head and tail rise. It did not seem to matter what height the river was either because they all used the short line regardless, but obviously altered fly size to suit conditions, although they rarely fished larger than a No. 6 in the Cemetery pool or the pools in the gorge upstream.

The fly fished on the waggled rod tip was another favourite method of that era and when I was a boy all the elderly anglers of the 1930s used this action automatically, and few used the handline technique that is so popular in the present era. Certainly it does give a lot of movement to the fly when a short line is fished, but the longer the line being fished the less effect the rod tip movement has on the action of fly, undoubtedly this is because the 18 inches to 1 foot up and down rod movement is soon absorbed by the elasticity of the modern line.

I must admit even today I am a great believer in fishing a short line whenever I think it can adequately cover the water I am fishing, and will probably wipe more people's eyes on this length of line than on the really long casting lengths. This is probably because I always religiously fan out my fly at the start of every pool, starting with the length of line that I have on my rod and casting it out I work it quietly on a rod tip angled square to the current, then lengthen a yard and do the same thing, until I have lengthened out to the length I intend to use as I fish down the pool. Only then do I begin to handline. By this method I cover every inch of my pool, whereas the angler who starts at the head of the pool and lengthens out line to reach across the width of the river before he actually begins to fish out his cast, misses all the fish that are lying within the 15–20 yard arc between the angler and his fly on the far side of the pool. It is really surprising how many experienced anglers are guilty of this careless error.

Another advantage that the short-line fisher has is that he is able to fish the nooks and crannies close into the bank he is fishing from far more thoroughly than his counterpart using a long length of line can do, and this painstaking search of the area is often justly rewarded. Certainly in the case of wide deep pools where salmon can lie across the full width of the river. I often fish the nearside of the pool down first with a short line, and then return to the head of the pool and start the pool again with a full length of line, and have always found that these tactics often pay handsome dividends.

There is also absolutely no doubt that in gorge pools, where the smooth surface of the pool is broken in many places by swirls caused by underwater ledges or rocks, the short-line fisherman is far more successful than his counterpart. Rivers like the Lower Shin, upper Beats of the Helmsdale, No. 1 Beat of the Lower Oykel above the Junction pool, the Alness, Lower Inver, and numerous other rivers in the north all lend themselves ideally to this technique. Especially on the Helmsdale, where the dibbled fly is much favoured, this technique can be just as effective when fished in similar fashion with just one sunk fly on the end of the cast.

Since the olden days when only one fly was the norm for salmon fishing, the dropper has become increasingly popular and is now used by many anglers during the summer months as a standard requirement instead of an exception to the rule. Anglers, therefore, who wish to practise this short-casting technique can also use a dropper if they wish. They then have the choice of either lifting the dropper to the surface at times and at others fishing it, as a wet fly fisher would for trout, submerged. This gives them another string to their bow and allows them to ring the changes of presentation of their fly according to conditions and with regard to the type of water they are fishing. Mainly using the surface dropper on the broken streamy heads of the pool and submerging it as the current dies.

Provided they make a careful approach to the pool and cause the least disturbance possible so as to ensure they do not frighten their quarry before the fish has time to see their flies, these short-line fishermen with barely more than their cast in the water can, by casting square and working their fly or flies by rod tip control back towards them, often pick up fish close to the bank in places where the ordinary long line fishermen rarely cover with their flies. These fish often take the angler's fly only a matter of feet from where he is standing, therefore he should try if possible to conceal himself, without of course impeding his casting ability.

Control of the Fly

Few anglers realise the advantage of being able to control the movement of a fly as it traverses across the width of a pool, sometimes
slowing down its movement and other times by hanging it over the
likely lies often denoted by an obvious boil or blemish on the surface
of the water, which assuredly means that there is a large rock, boulder
or rock ledge under the surface at that point. All too often one sees an
angler throwing a very pretty line at 45° downstream across the
current, and then putting his rod tip down close to the water with the
point of the rod facing almost directly downstream, thereby leaving
his fly entirely at the mercy of the current to control its movement
across the width of the pool, with complete disregard to any features
clearly shown on the surface of the pool. Other anglers often employ
the same type of method, but keep their rod tip at a much higher
angle, with more or less the same effect.

The first thing I do when I arrive at a pool, particularly if I have
seldom if ever fished the water before, is sit down at a vantage point
for a moment whilst I casually survey the pool I am about to fish. Not
only does this give me time to decide what fly I am going to use but it
also gives me a chance to assess the likely holding lies in the pool and,
probably more importantly, what method of presentation I am going
to use.

The main purpose of controlling one's fly or lure is to try and give
the fish the optimum chance of getting a clear view of it, and at the
same time present it in a lifelike and natural fashion so that the fish is
tempted into taking it. Instead of just casting the fly out and then
allowing it to flash across the width of the pool completely out of
control whereby the fish has hardly time to blink before it is past him,
let alone take it.

Fish generally lie on either side of the fast stream at the head of the
pool on the edge of the current, then as the main current disperses
across the full width of the pool, normally in strategic lies where the
velocity is baffled by some underwater object such as a large stone,
boulder or rock ledge. If there is sufficient current to flow throughout
the length of the pool, the tail of the pool can also be very productive
and often the draw where the water flows out is a favoured lie. A long
rod is probably the most important factor in giving the angler maximum control over his fly because then he is able to use its length to

slow down the movement of fly by holding his rod tip square across the current and then moving his rod tip downstream when he wishes to speed up its movement once again. The shorter the rod the angler uses, the less rod tip control he has over his fly, therefore, the more he must rely on mending his line across the current to slow down the movement of his fly, as this is the only alternative means of controlling the speed of traverse of his fly across the current. This method is useful when a floating line is being fished but when a sunk line is being used almost impossible to enact once the fly has settled firmly in the water, and in practice it is only feasible to carry out a quick mend coinciding with the moment the fly actually alights on the water. Naturally once again the longer the rod the more easily and efficiently the mend can be enacted.

Probably the fish that are most readily attracted to a fly are those that are lying on the far side of the river from the angler, this is mainly because the salmon has voracious feeding habits at sea and, therefore, being a predator this fish is more attracted by a lure going away from it, in other words trying to escape. It is, therefore, best to try and hold one's fly for a brief second as soon as it lands in order that fish lying in the vicinity of the far extent of the cast can get a clear view of it before it moves away from them. In order to achieve this control it is best to cast at 60° across the current and immediately move one's rod square across the current. This rod movement in conjunction with the angle of cast prevents the fly from moving instantaneously across the current, which would happen if the fly was cast at a perfect 45° angle across the current, and will even if you handline fairly fast hesitate for sufficient time to allow any fish in its vicinity to weigh it up and take it. Often I have caught fish by casting at this angle within a fraction of a second after it has landed on the surface of the water.

Having controlled the hesitancy before the fly begins its traverse across the current, I still keep my rod square to the current and handline quietly all the time in 6–9-inch draws until my fly has swung perpendicular to my rod tip. I then give three fast draws of 2–3 feet by handlining and at the same time move the point of my rod downstream to lead my fly further across the pool. The reason for the longer length of handline draws at this stage is to compensate for the rod tip movement downstream which naturally allows the line to go slack. Having led my fly right into the bank I once again move my rod tip square to the current before recasting, this final movement tends to move the fly away from the bank again out towards the centre of the pool and this often attracts a lackadaisical fish that has been following the fly into taking it.

Using a long rod to drag the tail fly on a glide

If, when I am leading my fly, I notice a swirl of water denoting a liking lie under the water, I once again square my rod tip to the current and hang my fly momentarily over the lie before allowing it to continue on its journey across the pool.

If there are promontories of land projecting out from the bank or stones protruding out into the pool on the bank one is fishing from, it often pays to get out on to these vantage points and hang one's fly momentarily in the centre of the current by use of the square rod tip technique. A long rod and use of vantage places are also invaluable when an angler is using the dibbling technique, and gives him much more control over his dropper tripping on the surface of the water. What I have described in this article is really nothing more than a different method of presentation and can be invaluable not only to search a pool more thoroughly but also to use as an alternative method when fishing a pool down behind another angler.

When fishing with a floating line I am still inclined to practise the same method of control but at the heads of fast moving pools I find it an advantage to mend immediately after the fly lands in order to make sure fish lying on the fringe of the current on the far side of the pool are given a fair chance of seeing my fly clearly before it moves away from them.

Extending a rod to hold a fly on the far side of the current

CHAPTER 4

SALMON TAKING

Salmon Behaviour Under Water Prior To Taking

There is no doubt that any angler who is experienced in fishing in gorges or off banks poised high above the river has often an advantage over the angler who fishes rivers flowing through flatter valleys or low ground, where wading is often necessary. This is mainly because the former, being poised high above his pool, is able not only to watch visually his fly working as it traverses the width of a pool, but also quite often the fish in their lies underwater as well.

This, quite frankly, adds a tremendous amount to the angler's enjoyment as well as teaching him many interesting facts such as how a fish moves to and takes a fly, how a fish lying in its lie reacts once the angler's fly lands on the water, and also how many fish actually move to the fly without leaving a tell-tale blemish on the surface of the water. All these fascinating sights, unfortunately, are lost to the angler fishing from water level who, until he feels a pull or a fish rises obviously to his fly, is quite oblivious to whatever happens under the surface of the water.

There is absolutely no question, I freely admit, that I have learnt a very large proportion of my knowledge about salmon and their taking habits due mainly to having the privilege of fishing from high stances, and I have not the slightest doubt that I owe a great deal of my success with a rod to this single factor. It has, for one thing, made me change my whole attitude to fly fishing especially when I am fishing at water level, my theory now is to bring fish up to the surface to my fly by using a larger light fly and fishing it fast, rather than trying to fish my fly deep nearer to the level that fish are lying at. My entire theory being, that it is better to make a fish move fast with impetus to a fly held high in the water, whereby he is bound either to take solidly if he catches it, and if he does not, he is then almost bound to leave a tell-tale blemish on the surface. I am then immediately alerted to the fact that I have moved a fish and can then try the fish again or make a mark on the bank and come back and try it later. Whereas, if I fish deep, my fly is much closer to the fish who then will only be moving slowly and cautiously as he approaches my fly and, therefore, often takes less solidly. If he misses the fly, however, I shall be completely oblivious of the fact that I have moved a fish, and will then naturally move on down the pool without giving the fish another chance to take it.

One of the more obvious facts an angler learns if he is in the fortunate position of being able to watch the fish which he is fishing over, is that the fish which is most likely to take is the one that is either lying higher in the water than the others, or the one that is moving around in the pool, even if the fish is making only the slightest movement. Those that lie completely inert in the water seldom, if ever, take.

It is also interesting to watch the fish immediately the fly lands on the water, because those that are interested perceptibly lower their tails and raise their heads ever so slightly, and those that are either coming to look at the fly or take it, will drift back downstream tail first for a few feet before making their move. Seldom, if ever, have I seen a fish come to take a fly before he has allowed himself to drop downstream, and if he has dropped station and does not take the fly, he normally does so the very next cast.

Once the angler hooks a fish and whilst the fish is being played, it is usual that the fish that were previously lying inert in their lies are disturbed. These fish will then mill around and move about the pool until the disturbance ceases, then begin to settle into their old lies. Personally, I believe in fishing the pool again as soon as I can after landing a fish, and on many, many occasions have caught another first cast. Other people argue that the pool should be rested for a while before fishing it again. However, this, in my opinion, is a fatal mistake as with all the fish alerted and none lying inert the angler is, on most occasions, assured of catching another, but within ten minutes many of the alerted fish will have once again gone into a trance and become inert again, and virtually uncatchable.

On numerous occasions in low water in a good holding pool I have found one either catches nothing or else several fish for this very reason, and on one occasion fishing with a No. 12 Blue Charm dressed on a long shanked hook, I took five salmon in five consecutive casts, and have had up to seven fish in a single fishing of a pool.

Provided salmon are not frightened or panicked into going deep and hiding under stones, minor disturbance to the extent of alerting them only does a lot of good.

In my long experience of salmon fishing, I can remember catching a 20 lb salmon on the Welsh Dee before breakfast, the very next cast after an otter had surfaced between me and my fly. I have caught fish in a pool minutes after bathers had got out of the pool, immediately after children had stoned a pool, and also in the same pool as a labrador dog was actually swimming in at the time.

I also knew one famed angler who used to get his ghillie to go up and down the pool with a lead weight attached to a length of blind cord, casting it in and pulling it out every two or three yards, before the angler would fish the pool. His theory was, 'What is the point of fishing a pool if all the fish in it are asleep? I want them to be awake so that they will see my fly', and in my experience there was a lot in what he said. In practice, it definitely worked, as he was a most successful angler.

Many times I have gone to a pool and seen all the fish lying inert alongside a rock ledge, and none would move to the fly. Having come back an hour or two later to the same pool and found one or two of these fish meandering about in it, I very often caught a fish straight away.

It is, I am certain, also the reason why in high water flows fish are much easier to catch. Admittedly, however, not when they are actually running, but when they begin to settle in a lie in a pool. If you watch these fish from a vantage point, they nearly always quickly explore the pool or tail of the pool according to the size of the pool, and having done so, then choose their lie, but even after some considerable time they are fidgety and extremely alert in their new environment. I would, therefore, assume that this is why they are more easily caught under these conditions.

Upstream Taking

This type of take in my early days as an angler was more to be associated with grease line fishing during the summer months, or once the temperature warmed up from mid-April onwards and size 6 downwards flies were being used.

I well remember a very old friend of my father's coming to fish for the afternoon at Argoed on the Welsh Dee towards the end of the war. It was early May just at the beginning of a very warm spell of weather, with the river dropping rapidly after a reasonable flood. There were plenty of fish in our beat and fresh fish could still move up river as the level was 6–9 inches above the height that would stop them running.

Mr Parker was very fond of grease line fishing and as I was only learning this method I suggested that I should go with him to the Summer House Run and Major pools whilst my father should go with the ghillie to try the Mill, Pentre and the Willow from the coracle. In spite of much persuasion I declined to take my rod as I was really interested in watching as I knew full well that Mr Parker was a very experienced grease line fisherman, and certainly a man who could give me many hints on this particular technique.

Having put on a very small March Brown dressed on a Tilson Hook, I watched avidly as he made cast after cast to perfection at 45° downstream and across the current, and then mended and remended whenever his fly showed the slightest sign of dragging. At last, about 15 yards below the pulpit, just on the far edge of the current, a salmon head and tailed at his fly and the angler with loose line in his hand never moved a muscle but merely remarked, 'He never touched me.' Three times this performance was repeated by three more different fish at varying distances apart further down the pool, still with the same result.

Mr Parker then changed to a similar sized Blue Charm, and fished the pool again, moving two of the four fish again in exactly the same manner and with the same result. In the Run he moved nothing, but in the neck of the Major he moved two more, the last of which turned as it took and drew the line out of Mr Parker's hand. On tightening I knew he was into a good fish and so it was, a fish just over 20 lb. After that, Mr Parker had to leave and having gone up to see my father, who was just landing in his coracle at the head of the Summer House Pool, he bade farewell.

After he had left I told my father about the fish his friend had risen and swore to the fact that I was sure several of them had taken the fly upstream but had ejected it before taking out the slack line, whereupon Mr Parker would have tightened on them. My father obviously doubted what I had said, and with a wry smile said, 'Well, you go and catch them whilst I watch because I have just caught two nice fish, one in the Pentre and the other in the Mill.'

Needless to say, I did not require any further persuasion and in no time at all I had my line greased and had attached a small low water March Brown to my 10/5 hercules gut cast. Knowing it was only about an hour before dinner time, I fished the head of the pool quickly as I had marked where each of the four fish had risen to Mr Parker very carefully. As soon as I cast over the first one up it came, head and tail onto the fly. As soon as the fish had disappeared below the surface I struck, and there it was firmly hooked, right in the back of the tongue as I found out when I landed it – a nice 12 lb. When I came to the next one, the same thing happened, hooked in exactly the same place – a 9 lb. Long before I reached the next fish, I had another head and tail rise, this time from a big fish and having struck, the battle was on. This time a 26 lb hooked as before, at the back of the tongue. I had, my father admitted, proved my point but it was now dinner time, and we had to go home.

As we wended our way up the red ash path that led us quietly back to the house as the quick way up the 232 steps was too strenuous for my father to tackle at his age, we discussed these last three takes, as my father wanted to know how I was so sure that they had taken Mr Parker's fly. I explained to him that when I had been at Rosehall the previous month, fishing the Cassley, we had also had very dry weather, and whilst fishing the Crows Nest from our usual stance, some 25 feet above the pool, I had had several fish head and tail onto my fly, take it in their mouths and then almost immediately eject it. I had been so amazed at the speed at which these fish ejected my fly that I found I had to strike, having so much slack line between me and my fly, as soon as the fish appeared on the surface.

That first experience on the Crows Nest was years ago now, but having found out the right timing of my strike I now very rarely miss a fish in this pool and every one that takes head on to the fly as the fish travels upstream, is always hooked in the same place, either right at the back of the tongue or in the roof of the mouth above it. I am certain this is because the fish is about to eject it.

Over the next few days at Argoed, both my father and I had tremendous sport on tiny flies practising this quick striking method on the upstream takers.

Not long after these incidents when I was spinning on the Dee in high water, I became aware once or twice of a brush on my line just as light as a leaf but no pull or anything else, yet somehow I felt I was no longer feeling the weight of my minnow on my pressure finger. The next time I felt this, I struck hard and sure enough it was a salmon hooked in the usual upstream take position. Since I first became aware of this, I have killed scores of fish both on minnow and on big flies fished on a sunk line, by striking as soon as I feel the brush, no matter how light it is. Naturally, when a fish comes upstream with your lure the line just goes slack, hence the slight brush.

The main point with this upstream take, either spinning or fishing the sunk line fly, is that you must be in complete contact with your lure and, therefore, it is best to have the line coming over your forefinger so that you are able to detect this faint brush or stop of the line, as it can be very light. When I am fly fishing I always handline, albeit slowly all the time, as this also helps me to detect it.

Another thing to remember when fishing either of these methods is that because you do not know how far the fish has moved upstream having taken your lure, you must strike much harder than usual in order to take up the slack line that this upstream movement has created, to enable the angler to have any chance for his strike to have the desired effect.

Certainly since we have begun to use large long winged and ordinary tube flies, the number of fish taking in the upstream fashion rather than the cross current take has, in my experience, increased vastly, and I would now estimate that nearly 50 per cent of my fish take in this manner in the spring time.

Whether this strange change in the salmons' taking habits, which was rare if not unknown in the early months of the year in the 1930–40 era, is one of the many unwelcome legacies brought about by the outbreak of UDN disease in 1967 must be a definite possibility, because this outbreak of disease and the main change over from large single iron flies to tubes or waddingtons with treble hooks, coincided almost together.

Other Types of Take

Apart from the fish that take a fly as they move upstream (which I have already described) salmon usually like to watch a fly carefully as it approaches and then, just as it passes they often move in towards the bank the fly is approaching and, having cut it off from the bank, they angle back towards the fly and take it crossways as they curve back to the centre of the pool where they were lying when they first spotted the fly. This is what I describe as the classic solid take and results in the angler feeling a firm pull on his line.

Naturally, the higher the fly is suspended in the water and the faster it is moving as it traverses the width of the pool, so accordingly the faster the fish has to move from his lie in order to intercept the fly and then return to his lie. There is no doubt, therefore, that the greater the impetus at which the fish is moving the more solid and definite the take must be. This in turn gives a far better chance for the fish to be hooked solidly as the impact of the take met with equal resistance from the angler (provided he is in contact with his fly) allows for maximum penetration of the hooks. If the angler chooses to deal with this type of take by giving the fish line instead of tightening immediately, the force and impetus of the fish will draw off this loose line and then tighten himself on the reel when the line is absorbed, which is much the same thing. The practice of giving a fish slack line when it took was originally devised to ensure the hook, once the fish closed its mouth on the fly, then slid in the fish's mouth and hooked the fish solidly in the hinge. There is no doubt this could and probably did work when a single ironed fly was being used because this type of fly would flatten on contact and could easily slide into the correct position in the fish's mouth. However, in the modern era when Esmond Drury hooks, trebles and doubles are the norm and singles the exception to the rule, these former three types are highly unlikely to slide anywhere in a fish's mouth once it has closed because one or other of the hook's points are almost bound to penetrate a membrane of skin, and anglers who allow fish to take out loose line now risk the fact that the fish may eject their fly if they do not tighten immediately.

Similarly, when the angler's fly is fished much deeper and, therefore, lower in the water, this type of taker will be travelling at a very much reduced speed as he makes contact with the fly. This is mainly because the fly is being fished at a level in the water which is much closer to the depth that the fish is lying at and he requires to use far less speed to cut the fly off from the bank it is making towards and intercept it as he returns to his lie. The impetus at the point of impact between the fish and the fly is, therefore, radically reduced. In this case, the angler who strikes is in a better position to ensure maximum penetration of his hooks, whilst the angler who gives line is in a much weaker position as the fish often lacks the necessary impetus to hook himself.

One of the other main types of takes is the fish that comes fairly quietly at the fly and snaps at it. This is a very difficult type of take to deal with because a fish taking in this manner is barely travelling at any speed at all, and often sinks slowly into the depths with the fly in his mouth, or alternatively, just catches it and ejects it almost in the same movement. Rarely, if ever, on these occasions does the fish turn with the fly in his mouth. It is, therefore, wellnigh impossible to hook the fish in the hinge, and fish taking this way, if they are hooked anywhere are normally lipped or else hooked right in the beak or point of the mouth. The angler in this case either feels just the stop of his line if the fish takes and sinks into the depths, or else a sharp pull if the fish snatches it. If, in the former case, he strikes immediately, he has every chance of hooking the fish solidly as with the fish's nose angled down, he should hook it either in the tongue or roof of the mouth, and if he is quick has a fifty fifty chance of catching the snatch taker if he is using a treble or Esmond Drury hook, but his chances on a single hook would be much reduced. The angler relying on the fish to take out his loose line in this case would have virtually no chance either way, as from lessons learnt through visual experience, even the fish that goes down with the fly seldom if ever turns, but instead drops back into its position in the pool tail first, whilst the others eject quickly.

The other very difficult take to deal with is the fish that takes virtually at the last gasp when the cast has almost been fished out, in other words, almost on the dangle. I have always found that if the rod tip is almost pointed straight downstream at the fly, fish are rarely hooked solidly but instead are nearly always lipped and with a couple of shakes of the head or wallows on top of the water, they often wrench themselves free. In order to counter this, I have learnt to lead my rod tip out towards the centre of the river again as my cast is virtually fished out, both to get a better angle for the next cast and hopefully to get a better hooking angle on these fish. Since doing so, I have had remarkable success with this type of taker. The angler with the loop can, provided the fish turns, also be successful with this type

Tying on the dropper – note the length of the rod

Manoeuvring a fish round a rocky outcrop

of take but much depends on the impetus the fish is travelling at at the time of impact once again.

When an angler is using a dragged fly on the surface in either the dibbling, riffling hitch or any other method, he must expect several new types of take, some of which are extremely gentle whilst others can be the opposite because fish may suck the fly off the surface or head and tail onto it, whilst others literally jump onto the fly with a great splash. I personally deal with all these differing takes by simply lowering my rod as the fish comes and then strike almost immediately, or else strike on any physical contact; otherwise the fish can, and often will, eject quickly. Some people prefer to let a loop of line go instead of lowering the rod and this can be effective too but I prefer to lower my rod in order to get a firmer strike from the body of the rod. Whereas if one lets line go one's rod tip remains at a high angle and the strike must inevitably come from the rod tip itself which after all is thin and flexible because its main purposes are to aid casting and be used as a buffet when fish are being played and certainly not to hammer a hook home and, therefore, often lacks the necessary power. This type of strike is more likely to embed the point and not the barb and infuriatingly with a shake of the head the fish will discard the hook with relief.

Anglers should always remember that if they are lucky and hit the soft gristle of the hinge flap, the soft tongue or roof of the mouth, all is well even with a relatively light strike, but the rest of the fish's mouth is hard membrane surrounding bone and this comprises a large percentage of the possible hooking area and needs a lot more power to penetrate and embed the barb which, after all, can be a considerable distance behind the point of the hook. A firm striker can drive his hook so that the barb is actually embedded in the jaw bone, but more often the point slides off the bone and the barb is then sunk in the tough skin surrounding the bone where it will remain safe provided this membrane does not tear as the fish is played.

UDN and its Effect on Taking

Many of us, who were lucky enough to fly fish for salmon prior to the outbreak of the disease known as Ulcerated Dermal Necroses, which affected salmon stocks in the United Kingdom from late 1966, fail to realise how fortunate we were to have had that privilege. I believe I can count myself to be luckier than most, because I was brought up on the banks of two famous rivers, the Welsh Dee and the Cassley.

Both during my youth and well on into my adult life, when I was at home on holiday or on leave, I was able to spend a large amount of my time on the banks of one or other of these rivers. Then, after my time in the forces, I moved up to live at and manage Rosehall Estate for my father, and during that time I spent some part of most days fishing the Cassley almost every day of the salmon season, from the 11th January to 30th September each year, apart, of course, for Sundays.

It was my experience over these years (up to 1967) that it was most unusual to fish the Cassley in any water height without an excellent chance of catching a salmon, provided one chose the hours carefully when you exercised your fishing effort in the less favourable conditions. In those days, before the advent of this damaging disease, one could kill numerous fish in April and May in the lowest of low water on a trout rod and greased line. Looking back through my records, I would be fairly accurate if I made a rough estimate that 50 per cent of the catch was killed in optimum water conditions, 15 per cent when the river was on the high side, and 35 per cent when low water conditions prevailed on a fly only beat.

However, once the disease struck, in June 1967, all this changed literally overnight. For the first few years it was really sad and almost distasteful to fish on many rivers because of the numbers of dead and dying fish which littered the banks and sides of the rivers. I think the sight of a beautiful clean fresh fish lying in the shallows or cruising close to the banks covered from head to tail (or in splotches) with fungus, took a lot of the fun and enthusiasm away from an angler, even before he had started fishing, although he still had a chance of catching a clean unmarked fish.

Naturally, the number of badly diseased or dead fish drastically reduced the amount of fish available for the angler to catch, but those that only had a touch of disease, or were unmarked, seemed to change their taking habits as regards fly fishing completely. Certainly in optimum conditions these fish, on occasions, did take reasonably freely, but as soon as water conditions were slightly off or weather conditions were adverse, the change was very marked. Fish not only became stiff to move or take but also those that did move to the fly either rose lethargically to it without touching, and would not come again, or they just plucked at it. Often shock tactics, such as using a ridiculously large fly, or in the advent of a quiet rise in water level suddenly happening, were on many occasions, the only hope of achieving success and these odd moments of glory seldom lasted any length of time, just in sporadic bursts.

Now, twenty years after the first outbreak, although dead and badly diseased fish are, for the main, a thing of the past, slightly marked fish are still in evidence during certain periods of the year and these periods can differ tremendously from river to river. Even though no marked fish are in evidence, in spite of the long lapse of time since the disease started, the free taking habits of salmon prior to the disease have never returned and fish, even today, only seem to take freely during optimum water heights and under favourable weather conditions.

Again from the records, since the start of the outbreak and up to the present time, I would estimate that nearly 80 per cent of the catch are killed in optimum conditions, 15 per cent when rivers are on the high side, and only 5 per cent in low water levels, a vast difference from the past.

Even during 1987, with excellent angling conditions prevailing for a lot of the season, the common complaint from all Scottish rivers was ideal conditions, plenty of fish, but few takers. Once again, although mortalities were negligible most rivers reported signs of UDN marked fish during some part of the season, therefore, it is extremely probable that it was this persistent disease which played a large part in upsetting the fish.

It would be very interesting to be able to quantify the actual loss of catch to rod angling that has been directly attributable to UDN since its original outbreak. Certainly from my experience, my guess would be at least a third of the catch as a conservative estimate, and probably more realistically 50 per cent of the catch as regards fly fishing. Probably on rivers that allow spinning or bait fishing, this figure could be slightly reduced.

Some people will argue that the increase of acidity in the water due to change of land use on the catchment of many rivers has had an appreciable effect on salmon taking. This I would agree with, but it would seem that catches have declined more drastically in the lower ranges of flow in recent years, rather than the higher ranges. This, therefore, would be more likely to be due to UDN, rather than acidity, as the latter effect would be more likely to be felt at times of high flow.

CHAPTER 5
WEATHER CONDITIONS

Dull, Cloudy Weather

This is probably the condition most favoured and sought after by anglers, provided the weather is fresh and not heavy and humid with thunder in the air. Most anglers venturing forth on this type of day know full well that try as hard as they may it will be difficult, if not impossible, to produce any watertight excuses for them to be able to save face if they are unsuccessful, unless of course, the river happens to be rising. This, therefore, spurs them on and they seem to try just that much harder and persist just that little bit longer.

Under these conditions anglers should choose a fly that they have confidence in of the right size, and just fish in their normal manner. If, however, this does not work they should then begin to think of a contrast and choose a fly that is likely to show up more than others against the forboding sky. I personally believe that a black fly fits the bill better than any other on that type of day, but also like to have a silver or broken silver body, or even a silver treble, to give my fly some form of relief. I also believe this body glints and glitters as the fly gyrates in the currents, and buffeting eddies, and this in turn attracts the fish's eye to the fly.

In the old days of the patterned flies, I used to favour the Mar Lodge, which was by far my most favourite pattern of all, or alternatively the Silver Grey, Dusty Miller or Silver Doctor, all of which were excellent flies in dull weather conditions. Now in the modern era, I would use a Collie Dog with its long black plume of hair wing dressed on a silver aluminium tube, ideally suiting this type of day. Or, if smaller flies were needed, a Stoats Tail or Silver Stoat or even a Hairy Mary, another of my great favourites which in all probability would, in these conditions, already be on my cast in the dropper position, as in the summer months after the water temperature rises to 42°F I always automatically fish with a dropper.

Other people, I know, swear by the Garry Dog or other flies such as the Yellow Peril, and Yellow Torrish, as they firmly believe that a yellow fly is good and shows up well on a dull day, and I would not disagree with that theory. Especially in the spring on the Welsh Dee in my youth, yellow was by far the most favoured colour, fished almost exclusively by the local experts and certainly it rarely failed on the duller spring days, even if the water was turbid.

Sometimes on these very dull days, espeically if the sun is trying to break through heavy cloud cover, it is common to get a very inky black light. This, I have often found, puts fish down. However, if you are lucky enough to have access to both banks, it often pays when this happens to change over and fish from the other bank, where the same problem seldom exists, and this very often makes all the difference with fish taking freely when presented with a lure from a different angle of light. It is simple tricks such as this, learned from experience, which often makes the difference between 'profit and loss' and saves a blank day.

Backing up a pool on a dull day is another of my favourite ploys as I find this method is eminently suited to these conditions, whether it is because the line is less noticeable or even the angler's presence on the bank, but there is, I am sure, some very good reason for it. Very often, especially if I have a lot of water to cover, I simply never bother to fish any pool down but instead back up every pool I come to, and this procedure has, I can assure you, held me in good stead for many, many years. It also saves endless time and in my opinion, certainly not at the expense of efficiency or thoroughness in covering your water, as it will take less than 20 minutes to back up a very long pool which would take over an hour to fish down.

The time saved, therefore, can be sufficient to fish three times as much water as one could otherwise do, and with good planning and careful thought this time can be used to the utmost advantage; either allowing the angler to return again (once or twice) to every pool, which I prefer to do, or alternatively, to concentrate on just one or two of the best.

Dibbling or fluffing a dropper or tail fly on the surface are all very useful methods of attracting fish on a dull day as the slight disturbance of these flies on the surface of the water is easily seen by fish even if they are slightly lethargic. In much the same way as the glint or glitter of tinsel alerts them, so also does this surface movement. Once alerted, fish move very fast to this type of attraction. I have often been playing my fly over fish I could visually see without effect; then lifted it to the surface, and caught one straight away.

I have met numerous anglers who in this type of condition believe that one should fish a slightly larger fly in order to give fish a better chance of seeing it. Quite frankly my experience is that this is not entirely true and I, if anything, err the other way and start with a smaller fly than I would normally choose, mainly because on this type of day there is nothing to impede their vision provided the contrast is right. To ensure that the fish is allowed to get the clearest possible view of the fly, it is important that the angler silhouettes his fly against

4. *A selection of old reels and single hooked Spring flies.*

5. *A well-stocked fly box and three old reels.*

the lightest background which invariably is the sky even though the clouds may be dark, therefore, the higher the angler holds his fly in the water, the more likelihood he has of achieving this very important factor.

In much the same way, anglers who fish in the late evening, almost at dusk, believe a larger fly is needed, but once again, except in the case of shock tactics as a last resort, I doubt their wisdom and I think fishermen experienced in night fishing for sea trout would back me up.

I suppose it is something to do with a boost to morale, if an angler believes a fish is absolutely certain of seeing his fly, but oh it is so easy to underestimate the sharp vision his quarry is endowed with and, therefore, to overestimate the size of the fly he needs to fish with, and I think that even the most experienced of us unwarily fall into this trap far too often throughout the entire season.

I remember being alerted to my misdemeanours in this field on several occasions in the summer time by trout fishermen. The two most glaring examples were on the Welsh Dee and on the Upper Shin. In the former case in May, I was fishing the Summer House Pool with a friend's son who was 8 years old and fishing for trout. Although I was fishing a No. 10 low water dressing of a March Brown I moved nothing all day but he, fishing a size 16 of the same pattern on his trout rod, was broken twice, fishing behind me, when two different salmon took his fly at different times of the day.

On the second occasion it was July and I and Willie MacKay had each fished the Ladies Pool for over an hour waiting for our host to join us, when a trout fisherman appeared and he immediately hooked two salmon within minutes on a tiny Black Gnat, both of which smashed his fine cast. We admittedly had fished nothing smaller than a No. 10 as this incident happened before tubes were invented. Both these happenings occurred on dark cloudy days without even a blink of sun.

On another occasion, in June on the Lower Cassley during a dull week with little water, a very keen tenant from Wales who had been blank for two days, showed me his fly box and sought my advice as to what fly to fish. In his box I noticed two size 16 double Peter Ross trout flies, and I suggested he should try these. He finished his week with three salmon (one of them 16 lb) and a grilse, all taken on these flies and lost another two due to the tiny hooks pulling out. Naturally he was well satisfied, but I wonder what he would have caught if he had kept to salmon flies for the rest of the week.

Bright Sunshine

Many anglers dread a bright sunny day with staring blue skies quite rightly, but are his chances really as bad as these conditions would signify? The straight answer to this question must be, firstly, this largely depends on the water height which prevails on that particular day, and whether there is a breeze stiff enough to ruffle the surface of the stiller parts of his pools. Naturally, if it is low water conditions his chances are materially reduced, but then he can avoid the worst of the relentless sunshine by fishing either before breakfast in the early morning before the sun is fully on the pools, or during the last hours of the day, as the sun begins to set and shade the pools.

If, however, he is forced to fish during the normal daylight hours, even then all is not lost in my long experience. As in everything else about salmon and salmon fishing, logic plays a very large part in helping an angler to achieve success. Therefore, an angler wants to pause and think carefully as to how much difference the actual angle that the sun lies in the sky makes to the angler's chances in regard to the pool he is fishing, or his choice of the time of day when best he should fish it. Many anglers, I am sure, would be better rewarded if they gave more thought to this factor.

On many, many occasions it is noticeable that as soon as the sun appears anglers scurry to their cars or to the fishing hut and immediately put on lighter casts and smaller flies, but is this always the best answer to the problem? Knowing how difficult it is to try and catch a cricket ball whilst looking straight into the sun, I have sincere doubts as to the wisdom about these seemingly wise precautions, but once again, this entirely depends on the angle of the sun in regard to the particular pool the angler is going to fish at that specific time.

It is well worth while remembering that in the main, when an angler is fishing a river flowing eastwards, the sun is shining from behind the fish and generally an angler fishing these east coast rivers need have no fear of his fish having to look into a ball of fire until later in the afternoon. Similarly, the angler fishing a west coast river is hampered once the sun has risen high in the sky, as fish in these rivers are then looking straight into it. It will, therefore, be well after midday before the sun has moved round far enough in the sky to clear the fishes' vision.

Regarding rivers flowing north or south, an angler will find that some pools on these rivers are affected, whilst others are not. Certainly anglers on these latter rivers, and pools situated in gorges or ravines, must learn when best to fish these either through bitter experience or else by guidance from their ghillies or fishing companions, because the angle of light can often suit some of these better in the morning than the afternoon, and vice versa.

It also pays dividends for anglers to think carefully and plan the order that they fish each individual pool on these sunny days, in order to try and catch the pools where he has the best chance of success before the sun's rays shine too relentlessly on it. Often it pays to fish only the most optimum parts of each pool so that he has time to move onto the next before the full sunlight hits it, then try the least productive places once the sun is affecting all the rest of his pools. In other words, fish lightly over the best places whilst they are still shaded or before the sun is too high in the sky, instead of wasting time on water that is already subjected to full sunlight.

Certainly in dead low water in the morning on east coast rivers and in the afternoon on west coast rivers, to tackle down and use fine tackle is eminently sensible, but in other heights of water it is best to use just the normal tackle and fly sizes which suit the conditions of the day, because when the sun is down river it makes little difference to a fish's vision.

I well remember in the late 1950s and early 1960s when the Cassley was dead low both my father and I, when we had bright sun and cloudless skies in the morning, used to use tiny low water dressings of March Brown, Blue Charm, Logie or Hairy Mary on fine casts and an American prototype Gladding floating line, which had a tiny metal eye fixed into the end of the line with a barbed bayonet-like spike. In those days, before the dreaded UDN disease reared its ugly head, we were assured of some of the most exciting sport, with fish taking freely like trout on an evening rise.

One morning I will never forget, in early April when the river had fallen fast after a spate due to hard frosty nights. My father went out at 10 a.m. in spite of the bright cloudless conditions and unfortunately, due to a meeting, I could not join him until 11.30 a.m. When I arrived at the Upper Platform, a favourite low water pool, I found him dejectedly sitting on the seat at the side of the large wooden platform, having not seen or moved a fish. As I tied on a tiny No. 10 Blue Charm, I saw a fish head and tail high up in the run at the neck of the pool. As soon as I tried for it, up the fish came and took. While I was playing it, I suggested to him that he should go up and try the Round pool, as I reckoned the fish were just waking up after the hard frosty night.

Having landed my first one, I unbelievably caught another four on consecutive casts, and when my father joined me to collect me for lunch, I found he also had caught four in the Round pool – a total of nine fish caught in under one and a half hours. Those were the days and I blame, rightly or wrongly, UDN entirely for the reason these days are seldom, if ever, repeated in low water at the present time.

In the mornings on the west coast and afternoons on the east coast, I believe that on pools where there is no relief to prevent fish from having to look straight into the glaring rays of sunshine there is still a chance for the ardent angler, who simply because of keenness will not give up, but he, in my opinion, must change his method of fishing almost entirely and resort to shock tactics. This is mainly because the chances of a fish being able to see a tiny fly neatly presented on a floating line whilst looking straight into a ball of fire are, to say the least of it, very remote.

Therefore, one must resort to other means to attract their attention. In medium to high water conditions I generally put on a large black fly, preferably of the long-winged variety, and back up the pools with it casting virtually at 90° across the river. In this manner I hope to strike the edge of the fish's vision outwith the ball of fire, and make my fly at the same time large enough to alert the fish of its presence. This trick very often works and even if the fish only rises to that size of fly, or even disregards it, if the angler fishes the pool with a reasonably sized fly immediately afterwards, the fish which has been alerted by the previous fly will often take it.

In low to medium conditions, I believe in either trailing my tail fly on the surface, or, in very low flows, dibbling. There is no doubt in my mind that these flies creating a disturbance on top of the water, are more likely to be seen under these difficult circumstances than the tiny submerged fly fished to perfection. I can also assure doubting anglers that this ruse does work on frequent occasions to a degree that it cannot be judged to be a mere fluke. Under these conditions I prefer to use a silver-bodied fly, so that over and above the surface disturbance there is an added chance of the glint from the body alerting a fish of its presence. But I freely admit that under the conditions when fish are forced to look into the full glare of the sun, an angler is really wiser to rest his water and try again when the sun begins to set in the sky late in the evening, unless water conditions are really favourable.

Especially in the early spring when days with blue skies, large white clouds broken from time to time by ferocious heavy rain or hail showers are quite common, are not ideal conditions for fly fishing, because of the glare on the water. However, anglers who watch carefully, and make sure that they are fishing good water, when the showers are shielding the sun or actually falling, will often find that everything changes during this often brief period, and they catch fish then. This also applies to snow showers as well, because when soft snow is actually falling the atmosphere warms up appreciably, and this can be one of the finest taking times of all.

Wind

Many fly anglers regardless of their experience in the art, seem to fear wind more than any other single element of weather condition. Rather than accepting the fact that wind is probably one of the greatest aids to a fly angler many regard it as an unwanted nuisance and make every excuse of the day to avoid going out and trying to overcome it, as they would willingly do if faced with any other adverse weather condition. The type of excuse one hears is 'fish never take when an upstream wind is blowing', or 'the wind is too gusty' and 'there are cats paws on the surface', 'the wind is far too cold, it will keep fish down and therefore they will not take'.

Certainly every angler would be untruthful if he did not freely admit that there are times when the wind can be troublesome, to the extent that it does seriously upset both the timing and smooth co-ordination of casting. The wise angler, however, keeps persevering even on these rare but annoying days and just has to use his experience to lessen his problem, by varying his casting techniques to meet the occasion or use his common sense and make for a more sheltered area on the beat. This may well mean changing over to the other bank if he is lucky enough to have access to it. Often the enthusiast will be duly rewarded for his persistence.

For every day that wind does really upset the apple cart and make the angler's task frustrating, there are many, many more days when it is an absolute blessing, being primarily responsible time and time again for making unfishable water fishable, by ruffling the smooth surface of the pool, or by freshening up close humid days which are hopeless for fishing, or by removing the menace of midges and insects. Even melting snow on the hills or hastening the passage of rain storms after a drought. If we face up to the facts, any experienced fisherman or ghillie will adamantly stress the fact that an airless, windless day, even early in the year when thunder is not present, is not good tidings for free taking and even the faintest, lightest whisper of wind can change this dour period into a bonanza.

There are also times when a hard frosty wind can act in reverse and suddenly put fish down after they have been taking freely. It is well worth just noting when a wind actually is beneficial and improves angling conditions. This is when it is sufficiently strong to ruffle the surface of a pool, thereby turning a still mirror-like pool with insufficient current to work a fly and therefore is quite unfishable, into a really fishable piece of water. Although much depends on whether the pool or the actual river one is fishing lies correctly to the prevailing wind (those flowing due east or west are better subjects and take wind more frequently than those flowing north to south) and in all cases with the proviso that the pools are not sheltered by cliffs, woods or high ground.

In a downstream wind as the wind is blowing with the current the riffle is not usually as pronounced or constant as is the case with an upstream wind blowing against the current, but it still can be quite sufficient to greatly increase the amount of fishable water available to the angler. This type of wind can ruffle a pool with a constricted tail far more than when the tail of the pool is wide and open.

The upstream wind is undoubtedly the most efficient at ruffling the surface and does not need to be very strong before it turns unfishable water into productivity. Naturally, the stronger the wind the more effect it has. Many believe that in low/medium river flows a 6-inch upstream wave is as good as a 6-inch rise in water, and I would heartily agree. Often fish lying in smooth areas of pools have not been fished over for some time and this, I think, adds to the reason why places like these are so productive once the wind renders them fishable.

Undoubtedly when still smooth areas of pools, which have insufficient current to work a fly, are ruffled by wind they should then be backed up and not fished down, as this method of fishing is eminently suited for fishing this type of water. The angler should start right at the tail of the fishable water and cast almost square across the pool, regardless of whether it is an upstream or downstream wind. He should then handline in and at the same time move quietly four or five paces upstream and cast again. This sweeps the fly right across the width of the river, and covers even the water close to the bank on the angler's side.

It is the impetus of the angler's movement upstream that trajects sufficient speed into the fly to enable it to traverse the width of the pool, as under these conditions there is insufficient movement of current to work the fly across itself. That is the main reason why backing up is so essential because fishing down the pool would be virtually useless, as the angler would have to inject impetus into the fly entirely by handlining.

When wind becomes a nuisance and impedes casting, there are many ways of easing the problem. Firstly, if an upstream wind prevents the angler from adequately covering his water, instead of fighting against it he would be far better to go down to the tail of the pool, quite regardless of the water height, and once again back it up. This he will manage with consummate ease as he is casting square across the wind. He should then just employ the normal procedure of this technique of fishing.

Many people know nothing about this method of fishing, others despise it, whilst others only apply it as I have described before, when a wind ruffles the surface of the water which has insufficient current to allow it to be fished down. I can, however, assure you that it is a most productive method under any water condition and I employ it on many, many occasions as a means of fishing a pool first time over in preference to the fishing down method. It has many advantages over the latter method as well as allowing one to fish the pool thoroughly in a far shorter time. One also loses far fewer fish this way, mainly because, I think, one is moving upstream away from the fly all the time and this necessitates that one is always in contact with the fly. Therefore, the line is always taut and one should feel any contact immediately no matter how light, and will be in a far better position to time the strike or tightening of the line correctly.

When the wind is bearing downstream on one's casting shoulder it is extremely difficult to time the back cast properly as the wind not only prevents it straightening out behind one, but also at the same time forces the fly downwards. In either case this makes it impossible for the angler to make a perfect forward cast.

To help cure this problem the angler can either cast wrong-handed where his back cast is being projected more across the wind than into it, so it is not nearly so badly affected. Alternatively, he can cast as I do, with the correct hand position for the bank he is fishing off, but taking the fly out of the water over his wrong shoulder and moving it upstream in a horseshoe movement, back around his head, and trajects it over his correct shoulder on the forward cast. Needless to say, this method is known as the 'horseshoe cast'. To my mind it is the perfect foil to the problem of the wind bearing down on the angler's casting shoulder and it is also the perfect cast to teach beginners, because it completely irons out one of the most common faults of all which is to allow the rod to go too far back when back casting, an impossibility with this cast.

Probably the most tricky incident to counteract is the gusty wind coming slightly upstream from a point just downstream of the angler and straight across the river. This needs perfect timing to conquer, and a slightly delayed timing is allowable as this direction of wind helps the angler to penetrate it by, strangely enough, helping to perfect the back cast. Whatever the angler does he must not allow

The Round Pool Falls on the Cassley

himself to be fooled into using forearm force to try to overcome this direction of wind as this simple, understandable fault will completely kill the penetration of the cast.

He must delay his cast instead and gently but definitely ease his cast through the wind turning his wrists at the last moment to inject the added power at the vital moment. Other anglers, quite wrongly, believe that this direction of wind can be better penetrated by use of the wrong shoulder cast but this is singularly ineffective. The result is rather akin to trying to penetrate a brick wall with a duster!

Finally, the cross river head wind, when the angler is standing below the level of the opposite bank. Being sheltered by the bank the angler himself often fails to realise the strength of the wind out in the open, and his overhead cast meets the full strength of the wind as it is projected forward many feet above his head. Once again, a definite, slightly delayed cast will ease the problem but under these conditions I usually use one of my own innovations, by using my rod in a scythe-like action, side ways on, I keep my cast protected from the force of the wind, below the bank level opposite.

Still, Quiet Weather

There is absolutely no doubt in my mind that these are amongst the most difficult which any angler can be faced with. Certainly the heavy humid conditions prior to a thunder storm breaking are without doubt as near useless as one can seldom, if ever, get a fish to take in the build up prior to a storm. However, once the storm has broken and vented its wrath over the locality, things can change quickly and dramatically.

First of all, the air clears and often a freshness can be felt almost as soon as the first drops of rain fall, and then it depends on whether the centre of the storm is upriver or downstream of the angler as well as its ferociousness, as to whether the river rises in a raging torrent, or actually rises appreciably at all.

I well remember two occasions on the Welsh Dee many years ago on the Argoed Water, when I was young and so full of enthusiasm that I was almost keen enough to fish in my bath!

The first was on a very heavy sultry day in June, with the water at an ideal level for the Pentre Pool. I fished the pool all morning without success and as it was the only pool I had to fish that day, Robert, the ghillie, and I sat down to eat our sandwiches on the bank. The sky got darker and darker to the north west of us, over the Ruabon–Wrexham area, downstream of us, and it was obvious the storm was about to break. As there was no fishing hut nearby, Robert pulled the coracle out of the river and placed it bottom upwards on the wooden cradle, about 4 feet off the ground. 'At least', he said, 'we will now have a roof over our heads to keep us partially dry when the storm does break.'

There literally was not a move on the surface of the pool, not even trout, coarse fish or parr dimpling the water and we had not seen a single salmon move for the last few hours, but I could see from Robert's expression he was not dejected. Then the thunder and lightning really started, but luckily we were only on the fringe of the storm which was centred several miles down river. Even so, the rain pelted down on the tarred felted coracle bottom above our heads and we watched the surface of the Pentre Pool as the heavy rain drops fell and burst on the water, almost reducing it to froth. Robert smiled, and in his musical Welsh lilt said, 'Soon we will get the fishes', and nothing more.

After a while the rain began to ease and a stiff downstream wind fluttered over the surface, and then the rain stopped. Robert quickly got up and launched the coracle, whilst I picked up my rod, and we were soon afloat. As we fished the double stone lie and moved into position to fish the five tree lie, I could see Robert was tense with expectation, and almost immediately my line tightened, and I had hold of a good fish. This one, unfortunately, got off as did the next one, but half-way down the pool I caught three, one after the other, all between 15 and 20 lb. As we landed the last one, my father arrived and I offered him my rod. After a brief argument, we swopped places and he caught a further two fish in the tail of the pool, but moved nothing more after I had gone home on his second time down the pool.

An afternoon to remember, in spite of the seemingly hopeless prospects in the morning.

On the other occasion I was fishing the Major Pool from the shingle on the left bank. This time the storm was two or three miles upstream, but we had an old hut in which to shelter. Robert turned to me long before the rain had stopped, and said, 'You had better start fishing as the river will rise. You will get soaked but you will catch a fish.' I duly did as I was bade and within ten minutes first rose a fish, and then caught an 8 lb fish. As I landed it, the river was rising appreciably. Robert quickly took the fly out of the fish, and told me to start again. Within three casts I hooked a big fish, and by the time we had landed it (a 24 lb) the place where I had been standing to fish the pool was under three feet of water and, of course, that was the end of the story for that day.

These two incidents go to show that it is still worth going out on a thundery day when a storm is brewing, because if one is not on the river when it breaks, one might easily miss these magic taking times, which even in the first case was not of lasting duration. Many times since I have had similar experiences on other rivers, and have always found that fish either take as the river rises, or for a short period after the storm breaks even if the river does not rise. However, never have I had success when the thundery rain is actually at its highest peak, although I do know of some anglers who have done so.

Probably the worst conditions of all are the really heavy sultry days, when no thunder storm materialises to freshen the air. This type of day I often link with the dog days at the end of July, when these conditions often prevail for three or four days on the trot. They can be extremely tedious, but one must just keep on trying and hope that a wind will eventually blow up and freshen the atmosphere.

An interesting thing I have found out on this type of day is that, having been blank all day, if one goes out again after dinner about 9 o'clock, even though it may still be very sultry there is then an excellent chance of catching a fish or two.

Strange to say, sea trout do not seem to be affected by these conditions in the same way as salmon, and if one catches some of these too, it is always a bonus.

It is also quite common throughout the entire season, to get a number of completely still, airless days without a breath of wind but with no semblance to sultry thundery weather. It would seem to most people that these days would be absolutely ideal for angling, as the angler is on these occasions able to place his fly almost anywhere at his will's desire. However, in my experience this type of day can be extremely disappointing with fish often dour and difficult to move. During this type of weather, especially during the summer months, anglers are not only frustrated by the stiff behaviour of the fish, but also nearly demented by the vicious swarms of midges or black flies, and in no time at all are literally praying for a wind, even though it's a gale, to get up and rid them of these unwelcome pests. It is quite strange how, when the wind does rise, fish come out of their doldrums and seem to take freely again, almost as soon as it rises.

So once again, as in many other aspects of salmon fishing, patience is the essence of success, and those who have it are generally rewarded, while those who do not miss many a highlight in this unpredictable sport.

CHAPTER 6

WHEN TO FISH

Before Breakfast

This is certainly one of my favourite times to fish from mid-April onwards. Not only is it one of the most tranquil periods of the day before, with a hustle and bustle, the countryside becomes awake, but also a bewitching hour to study wildlife just before the nocturnal wanderers return to their hide-outs for refuge during the daylight hours.

Quite apart from the solitude, it is also one of the most productive periods for an angler to venture forth full of confidence. I think the main reasons for this period of the day being one of an angler's best chances are really very easily explained, and once again it is a combination of circumstances and not by any means due to one main factor.

The fact that fish have not seen a lure during nightfall is probably one to be taken into account, but more importantly the fact that many of these fish have in all probability moved pools or their lies in the pool overnight and at that hour may still be on the move, is of far more significance. Except in the lowest of low water flows, during the months that early morning fishing is possible, there is nearly always a significant movement of fish during the hours of darkness either as they ascend up river or else within the pool itself, as water temperatures have by this time of year risen to the mid 40°F or above. With these higher range of temperatures, because salmon are a migratory fish they are restless to ascend the river system to the proximity of their spawning grounds before relaxing and biding their time until they themselves are ripe to spawn.

This instinct to keep moving forward up river means that they are prepared to take advantage of any reasonable height of water to ascend some distance upstream whilst in lower flows, they are quite prepared to move even slowly at the rate of one or two pools every night.

This is probably one of the main reasons why the angler who gets up early has an advantage over those who begin their fishing after breakfast because by that time of day, in the lower range of flows, fish movement will have ceased and in many cases fish that were a few hours before in the most likely taking places such as shallow runs or in the streamy necks of pools have, a few hours after sunrise, fallen back into the deeper stiller areas of the pool often where a fly is unfishable due to lack of current.

Another factor in favour of the early bird on the river is the correct balance between water and air temperature, i.e. that the water temperature is lower than the air, particularly in low water flows. In the early morning the water temperature is at its lowest ebb after the cool of the night, whilst the air temperature after sunrise is rising quickly, therefore, during the first few hours of daylight it is highly probable that the air temperature is appreciably higher than that of the water, providing perfect conditions for good taking, whereas within a matter of hours all that is in favour of the early fisher may be destroyed for the after-breakfast angler if perchance a cold wind happens to get up, which could so easily lower the air temperature significantly, a thing that is on balance highly likely in our present summer climate.

The after-breakfast angler can also get a large part of his angling period ruined by bright sunlight, whereas the early bird seldom, if ever, is embarrassed by this problem, because even if the sun is bright, he will usually find some of his pools well shaded at this hour.

Mist on the water is more likely to be a problem at this hour of the day, but this usually disperses fairly quickly and I have on occasions caught fish with mist on the water in the early morning, but rarely when it is falling in the evening.

I have always found the very neck of the main pools, shallow runs or runs and the tails of pools particularly productive at this early hour, but my advice would always be for an angler to fish his whole beat down quickly but efficiently rather than concentrate on one particular place. He then has a much better chance of finding a fish that has changed pools or lies overnight, and if he does, this fish will often take.

Even in the higher ranges of river flow I still believe that the early bird has a huge advantage over the angler who keeps to regular daytime hours, not only are wind and sun rarely a problem at this time of day, but also fish are beginning to settle after their night time exertions at this hour in lies they have often just occupied, as well as the fact that he is getting the first crack of the whip, being first on the water.

Having come in for a break, and refreshed by breakfast, he can then if he so wishes, fish on till lunchtime or 2 p.m., and then have the afternoon off, and fish again in the evening from 5 p.m. onwards or later, according to the time of year. In the main I have always found the hours between 2 p.m. and 5 p.m. the least productive period after mid-April, and up to early October, but there are always exceptions to this rule. If for example, a rising river begins to hold and drop just at this time of day, or a wind gets up in the afternoon and ruffles flat water previously unfishable, or even a run of fish happens to come into the beat and rests during these hours, so one can never be too specific over these matters. In the long run there is no doubt that it is the angler who keeps his fly in the water longest who, at the end of the day, ends up the winner. Whether he is ever really fully rewarded pro rata for his efforts, is another question.

In the lowest flows, there is little doubt that the wise angler is more likely to be rewarded if he flicks his water over before breakfast, and again at dusk, whilst during the main hours of the day he finds some other form of recreation. In this way he avoids hammering his water when conditions are usually just about hopeless. Then fish that are rested for the main part of the day often take when they are in the more favourable areas of the pool at dawn or dusk.

To sum up, I have no doubt that this period of the day's main advantages over the normal daylight hour period are mainly based on the fact that in the early hours fish that have been moving, or trying to move pools overnight are still in the streamy necks of pools or in shallow runs at this hour of day. These fish are, therefore, in the optimum taking places where the fly angler has the best chance of catching them. They are also likely to be alert and attentive in this environment, whereas a few hours after sunrise many of these fish, in the lower flow ranges, will fall back into deeper less streamy lies where they are more difficult to catch on the fly, whilst in the higher flow ranges these fish will be tired after their overnight activity and will lapse from alertness into inertness, as they rest their weary muscles and often for the next few hours are virtually uncatchable. These facts are, therefore, stacked in favour of the angler who ventures forth early.

Similarly, the weather conditions as well as the vital favourable air and water temperature gap are almost inevitably, as I have pointed out previously, in the early angler's favour, which once again gives him a considerable advantage. Whereas a few hours after sunrise, climatic conditions can change drastically, and this change is unlikely to be in the angler's favour.

Another small point to be considered is that problems such as vibration are also seldom troublesome at that time of day. Things like blasting in the local quarry, low-flying jets shattering the tranquility of the day with the roar of their engines, even tractors working in nearby fields, are all the more likely to be troublesome later in the day. Even children paddling or bathing in pools, throwing stones in the water or otherwise causing disturbance or tourists impeding casting seldom cause disruption at this early hour. All these are, admittedly, minor nuisances but none the less important especially in low water.

Ordinary Daytime Hours

Many people often ask the question as to which is the best taking period during a normal daytime fishing period, and this is a very difficult question to answer, mainly because there are many factors which have a definite bearing on the subject.

If, however, one takes the case that the river is settled and dropping, and weather conditions are favourable with a good stock of fish in the river, and study that situation first as a basis on which to found the argument, and then study the other factors later, it may be possible to produce a reasonable answer.

Naturally, first thing in the morning, when the pools have been rested overnight and fish have mainly settled down after overnight movement, there must be an excellent chance of catching fish settled in their new environment. Therefore, the first or second fishing over each good holding pool must be an excellent chance, and I have no doubt that on the Cassley and many other rivers that I know well, a large number of fish will be caught the first time the pool is fished over that day, but not all pools will be fished for the first time at the same time of day. Therefore, this benefit will in all probability be spread out throughout a large part of the morning, and even into the afternoon in some cases. This often makes some people confuse the time when they catch a fish first time over a pool with a good taking time and this may not necessarily be true, but just the fact that they have found a fresh fish which has moved into the pool overnight, or a stale one which has moved pools overnight. In both cases these fish, settled in a new environment in one of the best taking lies in the pool, can often be readily taken when the pool is first fished over, regardless of the time of day.

What we are really looking for is a time of day when fish which have been actually fished over before that day, come on the take.

From years of experience of studying this aspect, I have always found that between the hours of 12 noon and 2 p.m. fish often seem to wake up and pools that have seemingly earlier in the day been devoid of fish, frequently become alive. Some people pass this off merely as a run of fish suddenly entering the pool, but as it also happens in low water when fish cannot run, I seriously doubt whether this assumption is always correct, although it could be the reason on some occasions.

Certainly I know when I am fishing with friends I always insist on

Dibbling the Round Pool Pot

staggering the lunch hour so that some take an early lunch, and others a late one, to ensure that there are rods on the water during this whole period. I think this results from my youth, as my father was a most punctual man and insisted on us all leaving the river at 12.50 p.m. so that we could be home for a prompt lunch by 1 p.m. The number of times one or other of us, including him, would hook a fish just as we were finishing off our last few casts was quite uncanny over the years, and I know that since I started fishing through the lunch hour this has paid me handsomely on many, many occasions. I remember several times killing four to six fish during this period, when my companions had not even moved a fish earlier in the day.

Many people will ask, quite rightly, why should this be? I myself do not believe it is coincidence, but merely the fact that fish which have been moving pools or even around pools during the night, often lie inert for most of the morning, but, especially in good water flows, wake up about mid-day prior to continuing their journey upstream in the afternoon. These fish, therefore, are likely to be alert and eminently takeable as they begin to prepare for the next stage of their migration upstream, and this I am certain, explains why these hours can be one of the best taking periods of the day.

Between 2 p.m. and 5 p.m., fish can often become far stiffer to move especially in the main lies of the bigger famed holding pools, and I have often found this period amongst the most unproductive of the day. However, there is one reservation I must make, and that is it often pays to forget about the main holding pools during these hours, and fish instead the shallower pools, runs and resting places in between the better recognised holding pools, as this is where it is far more likely an angler will be able to intercept fish which are on the move in shallower areas where, if he finds them, they will often take far more freely. As salmon are gregarious creatures, they normally travel in small groups of up to six or more, and if an angler is lucky enough to find such a group resting, he can often catch two or three in what looks like a fairly insignificant place.

The reason for exploring these less renowned resting places in the afternoon is that fish which moved into the river or changed pools during the night, have rested during the morning and then begin to push on again during the afternoon. Those that have similarly moved during the morning, often lie inert in a trance in the main holding pools during the afternoon and are, therefore, difficult to catch.

After five o'clock fish once again start to think of moving on as the hours of darkness begin to approach, and from that time on until dusk fish are on the whole more likely to take as they become alert, in preparation for their night's activity, and because of this are far more attentive. It is, therefore, well worth the angler concentrating his efforts during these latter hours of his fishing period on both the main holding pools and runs and resting places alike. When I am fishing beat three of the Lower Oykel, one of my favourite haunts when the river is in good order, is the Dyke pool sited midway. between the famed holding pools known as the Brae downstream and the Langwell upstream. During these hours, in the late afternoon and evening, I have often had great sport as fish moved out of the Brae bound for Langwell, very often catching fish in this pool when other rods fishing elsewhere on the beat were not even getting a touch.

Especially in the spring, when darkness falls early, the last couple of hours of daylight can be by far the most productive of the whole day and many refer to these hours as 'the magic taking time'. It must be remembered, however, that this is often helped at this time of year by a gentle rise in water level during the late afternoon, due to snow melting on the hills, if the day has been mild or sunny. This, in turn, excites fish and obviously makes them both alert and attentive and, therefore, is an added benefit peculiar only to this particular time of the year.

Apart from this rough guide to the best taking times, and where to look for fish at different times of a normal 9 a.m. to 6 p.m. daytime fishing period, anglers must, of course, bear in mind that there are certain factors which can disturb this regular pattern. The most important of these is, naturally, the presence of fish in the beat one is fishing, and of course, if a run comes into a beat that has been practically devoid of fish, the arrival of these (provided they rest in the beat) can cause fish to suddenly to take freely at any time of the day.

Weather and water conditions can also interfere with the regular taking times. For instance, if the river begins to rise fast, as the first fresh water comes in fish will take freely for about half an hour, but unfortunately this magic moment is so short that there is only time to hook or land one or at the most two fish, before it is over. For the rest of the duration of the rise an odd fish may be caught but more are likely to be lost or pulled as they seem to take short when the rise is on. However, once the river settles and begins to drop, fish will start to take freely again because one slowly dropping after a rise in water is the most favoured for angling.

It is interesting to note that a gentle rise, such as from snow melt, seems to incite fish and they will normally take freely during this period, even if the river moves as much as three to nine inches in an hour, and are not put off the take by this type of rise as they would usually be.

Thunder or sultry conditions, as well as gusty windy conditions when 'cats' paws' run in scuds across the surface of the water, are all unfavourable for angling, and generally put fish completely down. On the other hand, soft snowfall can be an excellent taking time even if the snowstorm almost blacks out the light, this is probably because as the snow actually begins to fall the atmosphere warms up appreciably.

It is also strange that an airless day without a breath of wind when an angler can literally cast a fly at his will, even if there is no sign of thunder about, is seldom good for free taking and yet often on these occasions if perchance a gentle breeze or stronger wind rises, they will frequently begin to take freely almost straight away.

So, quite apart from the normal regular pattern of better taking times during the day, any one of these factors can disturb this and thereby create a false pattern on that particular day. However, the experienced angler will know the reason for sudden bursts of unusual activity, whilst the optimist will just keep plugging away full of enthusiasm and probably by keeping his fly in the water regardless of weather and water conditions, in the end he will be the most successful of all of us. The beginner, however, will lead himself quicker to success if he largely follows logic and, at the same time, assimilates all the information he can glean for himself, as he will find this invaluable over the years and long into the future.

In the Evening

Once the clock is put forward an hour in late March and British Summer Time begins, anglers begin to look forward once again to fishing in the evening. This time has, and always will be, a very favoured period of the day for both trout and salmon fishers albeit for different reasons, the trout fisher because his quarry often comes on the feed and rises more freely at that time of day, whilst the salmon angler feels his chances of catching the wily, unpredictable salmon are often better late in the day and very often he returns home successful and well satisfied at being rewarded for his efforts.

Why, therefore, when salmon are not supposed to feed on their return to freshwater is this particular time of day very often a good time to catch salmon. I believe this results not from one particular reason, but instead a combination of circumstances caused mainly by both climate and fish movement.

Invariably, as the day draws to a close the wind often falls in velocity and with this change the air warms appreciably, even in the summer time. This in turn often allows the vital temperature gap between air and water temperature to rise appreciably in favour of the air. This, especially for fly fishing, is a very important factor as salmon rarely, if ever, take when the water is warmer than the air and although a nil gap is acceptable they tend to take far more freely as the air temperature rises a few degrees higher than the water temperature. At the same time as the evening draws to a close if it has been a sunny day, the sun begins to get low in the sky and more and more pools become shaded from the glare, and, therefore, much more fishable. If an angler knows his water well he will know on sunny days which pools are shaded first as dusk approaches and be able to plan accordingly, so that he fishes these pools early in the evening and leaves the last pools to benefit till the last possible moment. If he fishes a pool before it is properly shaded he may do more harm than good by disturbing fish that might have been takers a short while later.

If he is fishing water set in deep, narrow gorges, it is sometimes wise to fish the narrow shut-in pools earliest in the evening and leave the wider pools and those more favourably angled towards the light till the last, intimate knowledge of this type of water is a priceless asset as even during the day time some pools set in gorges fish better in the morning than they do in the afternoon and vice versa, normally entirely due to light. I know of one famed gorge pool that kills around 100 salmon in a season, where no salmon has ever been known to be taken after 7 p.m. even during the height of summer although it is always full of fish at all times of the day and, for that matter, night.

Another important factor that must be borne in mind about evening fishing is fish movement. Fish, particularly when the water levels are beginning to drop to summer level, rest mainly during daylight hours, and move on during dusk and during the night time, except over formidable obstacles such as falls which they have to jump in order to ascend them. In this case, whereas evening up to dusk is a much favoured period to ascend them, once darkness has actually descended all fish movement ceases at these points.

With this tendency of fish movement to increase in the evening, it also follows that fish which have been lying in deep, slow moving, unfishable areas of the pool during the day now move into the streamy heads, necks and tails of the pools in the evening, either as they prepare to move on upstream or in the act of doing so. This makes them eminently more catchable as they now frequent the most fishable sections of the pools where the angler's fly can be presented to the best advantage, and those that are either preparing to move on or have just entered a new pool often take freely, having changed their lies. Even good taking lies that have been occupied by a wily old stale fish for several days are often vacated at this time of day and the angler, therefore, has every chance of catching the new occupant of this lie.

This pre-dusk fish movement is a far less hurried operation than the wholesale ascent of fish upstream, which occurs normally when the first spate after a long period of low flows takes place, then running fish are so keen to ascend the river that they simply disregard any lure presented to them, and are virtually uncatchable unless the angler finds where they are resting on that particular day. This is the reason why evening fishing can be so productive.

In higher water flows when fish are ascending the river freely during daylight hours very often towards dusk these fish begin to slow up and very often rest at this time of day before continuing on their journey later during the hours of darkness. Once again even during February, March and April from 4 p.m. onwards to dusk is often one of the best taking periods and as the hours of daylight grow longer so also does this magic taking period get later in the day. Often in the higher water flows it is the tail of the pool or centre body of the main

Using the square rod position to fish The Run

Fishing broken water

pools that can be the most productive, but even in these flows the quiet water just on the edge of the fast current in the very neck of the pool can be a very useful taking place, as fish often pause here briefly, before making their final ascent through the rough high velocity throat of the pool as they move on upstream in search of their next resting place.

CHAPTER 7

PLANNING A DAY

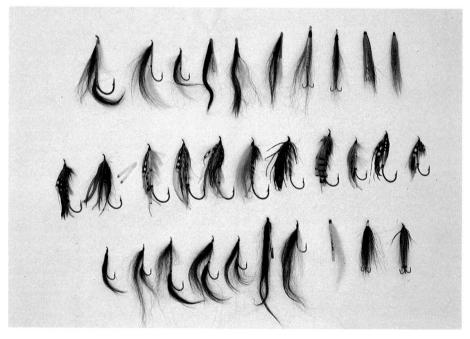

6. *A selection of Collie Dogs and Tadpoles, and (below) modern long-tailed flies and old Spring patterned flies.*

The Choice of a Salmon Fly

When an angler arrives on the bank of a river at the start of a day's fly fishing for salmon, the first question he must ask himself is what fly shall I put on?

There are many aspects to be considered before the angler goes firm on his final selection, as this choice can literally make or mar his day's success. It is, therefore, worth pondering over this interesting question in order to decide whether there are any essential criteria, that, if studied carefully, can guide an angler into making the correct choice which will enhance his chance of catching fish on that particular day.

There is no doubt that if an angler has the benefit of local knowledge, he can often be guided by either the ghillie or a friend to fish with a certain pattern of fly, which for some reason or other is much favoured in that locality. It is a fact that wherever one fishes throughout the UK, it is rare to find an area that either does not favour some bastard pattern of their own or else a particular pattern of the many well-known named varieties.

However, before deciding whether it is wisdom on his behalf, just pure luck, chance or local knowledge that leads him to make the right decision, it often pays him to study the following points carefully–

1. Is it the size of fly that matters most, or
2. Is it the colour that is most important?
3. Is it the composition of wing, hackle and body?

I personally believe that it is a combination of all these aspects that, if given due consideration by the angler as he selects his fly during the varying seasons of the year and the wide variation of water heights that he is often faced with, can help him to greatly improve his chances by making the right selection.

Before going into the above points in more detail it is perhaps wise to ponder briefly on the feeding habit of our quarry. We know that a smolt migrates to sea 3–5 inches in length and a mere 1½–3 oz in weight. We know that after spending only one winter in the sea it returns as a grilse and weighs 3–12 lb, but if it remains two or more winters at sea it returns as a salmon weighing anything from 6 lb to 40 lb. We are left in no doubt therefore that during their feeding period at sea, salmon are voracious feeders and if they were allowed to continue these feeding habits on return to freshwater, they would decimate other freshwater fish stocks, including their own species, in their rivers of origin. Nature, therefore, allowed for this fact and has given them the ability to survive on a complete fast on return to fresh water, if they are required to do so. The prime and sole reason for their return to fresh water is for the purpose of regenerating the species.

The very fact that these fish do not have to feed daily in order to sustain themselves, the same as any other freshwater fish, obviously makes their taking habits completely unexplainable and unpredictable. This is probably why salmon fishing fascinates so many anglers, the very fact that the quarry has such unpredictable taking habits is a real challenge to many ardent anglers. Salmon can, however, at times be very easily caught whilst at other times they are the very opposite, virtually uncatchable.

There is no doubt that weather, water conditions, and air and water temperatures play an important part as to when salmon are catchable, or not, on a fly. Optimum water conditions to suit the actual beat one is fishing is undoubtedly the most important factor of all concerning salmon taking. Not only does this improve the chance of actually catching fish, but it also draws fresh fish out of the sea or moves the resident stock in the pools lower downstream, into the beat. Sea-liced fish, provided they are resting in the pools the angler is fishing, usually take freely but so also do stale fish which have only moved pools due to rise in water. Fish that have been resident in a pool for a matter of a few days soon get stale and are then more difficult to catch with a fly than those that have just arrived and are resting, running fish seldom take.

Often small resting pools or runs where fish literally only remain for a matter of hours can be amongst the most productive for the fly fisherman, whilst pools that are crammed full of fish can be at times the least productive.

Water temperature is probably the most vital factor of all, with the water always requiring to be at a lower temperature than the air. A 5–10°F gap between the two is ideal and this type of gap is frequently found in the early spring, mainly due to winter snow melting on the high catchment areas and night frosts keeping the water temperatures down below the milder air temperatures. Once again in the autumn, with increasingly longer hours of nightfall, more rain and the odd early touch of night frost once again make the water temperatures drop quickly. Undoubtedly, both the spring and autumn periods give more consistent results to the fly fisherman. During the summer months, particularly when there is a lack of water, the temperature gap is often non-existent or even at times the water is warmer than the air, and therefore anglers chances are much reduced. It is during these periods that the angler who is willing to get up early before breakfast often scores. Conditions then are more likely to produce the right gap between the temperatures, with the water at its lowest after the cool of the night and the air rising rapidly after sunrise. Evenings can also be productive in these conditions, but this time of day normally provides a less favourable temperature gap. However a good rise in water often eases the problem, and it is during a spate or as the spate runs off that the summer fisherman will have most success.

Weather conditions also affect good taking, for instance, when it is either sultry or thundery salmon seldom take, and a heavily falling weather glass can also be detrimental to good taking. On the other hand whilst snow is actually falling in the spring it can be one of the finest taking times I know of, but frost falling in the evening can be fatal and quickly puts fish off the take.

If salmon do not have to take daily on their return to fresh water in order to sustain themselves, then it is reasonable to suppose that those that do fall prey to anglers have had a memory from their feeding habits at sea and have been lured into making a mistake which often proves to be fatal! We, therefore, turn to the points I have stressed earlier in this article and study them in the same order as I listed them.

1. *Size of Fly*

There is little doubt that this is allied to water temperature in the river. In water temperatures ranging between 34°F to 42°F salmon favour a fly 1½–6 inches in length, varying according to river flow and depth at which it is fished. In temperatures from 42°F to 50°F, salmon are less choosey and can fall prey to flies ¼–6 inches in length, again varying with changes of water height and depth. During summer months, however, with temperatures varying between 50°F to 65°F salmon are far more selective and favour a much smaller fly, ranging from size 16 to size 4, for the most part, except in high water.

This virtually means that in early spring and late autumn large flies are the order of the day. Late April to mid May and again mid September to mid October, an angler should ring the changes over a wider range and in the height of the summer concentrate on the very small fly sizes. There is no doubt that during this latter period most anglers are inclined to fish with flies that are too large such as size 4 or 6, when size 8 or 9 would be better.

The angler should, however, never rely on any golden rules passed down either as heresay or inheritance. If educated to the art he relies on fact he has learnt through persistence and his own experience. Although wisdom will always make him test out the 'golden rules' for himself before deciding whether they are, in fact, fact or fiction, normally he will find that these rules are well thought out, although interpretation sometimes tends to distort them. This angler will be the man who is thorough and tries on his best holding pools first the fly he thinks is the right size, then something sublime and then the ridiculous, to make sure he has offered his fish every chance to make that fatal error. Very often he will be the man who confounds the experts and catches fish when others do not!

2. *Colour of Fly*

Many people firmly believe that salmon are colour-blind and quite frankly laymen in the field, like myself, are in no position to argue this fact expertly because we simply have not the knowledge, though experience in fishing for many years leads me to seriously doubt this fact.

When a fly is fished high in the water it is what I call being fished in the fishes' window. In other words, it is silhouetted against a background of the sky, quite immaterial as to what weather conditions prevail on specific days. Obviously a fly will show up clearly against this background, regardless of cloud cover or brightness, but whether as it twists and buffets through the uneven currents and eddies close to the surface of the water, it is possible that the fish can distinguish differing colours, it is really impossible to say for sure. However, when the fly is being fished deeper, closer to where the fish is actually lying in the water, the fish no longer can contrast it against the sky but against the contour of land, river bank or underwater rock. Also in this case it is more than likely that this contrast has to be made through a wall of water which either is turbid or peat stained for much of the year, and differing colours may well be an important factor under these conditions.

Through sheer experience and nothing else, in my mind there can be little doubt that yellow and silver colours are more effective in the spring months, maroon and drab colours during the summer, and orange undoubtedly the most effective single colour during the autumn months. Black, however, seems to have become the most favoured colour in recent years and is used extensively throughout the whole fishing season by many anglers.

Fishermen who use the more gawdy colour ranges when there is turbidity or peat stains in the water have more success and this may well partially account for yellow being favoured in the spring time and orange or red in the autumn. However, during the early spring when rivers are running absolutely gin clear due to the snow melt, yellow flies can be great killers. Similarly in early October or even in November, long after the peat-stained water has cleared, orange or red flies amongst others are prominent in most game books.

3. *The Wing, Body and Hackle*

For many years fly tiers took infinite trouble to tie most elaborate, patterned flies such as the Jock Scott, Mar Lodge, Childers, Red Sandy and countless others, to the minutest detail without one correct feather missing in the wing. In all probability, however, as much care and attention went into the actual body of the fly or as to whether the pattern deserved to be dressed with jungle cock feathers either side of the fly, just behind the eye, or whether there should be a pronounced hackle at the throat, or a more subtle hackle slightly veiling the body of the fly. There is little doubt that this minute detail was inserted into these flies for a specific reason and not just for window dressing. The jungle cock for instance undoubtedly was there to imitate the eyes of a fish and was to be found in nearly all the most favoured spring patterns.

It is interesting to note, however, that it was nearly always omitted from the most famous summer flies, such as the Blue Charm, Lady Caroline, Logie, March Brown, or Silver Blue, but at the same time was nearly always found in the various patterned shrimp flies.

Hackles were without much doubt inserted to inject more movement to the fly, opening and shutting as the fly negotiated the varying buffeting currents and surface eddies as it traversed the width of the river.

Bodies of silver or gold, some plain, some ribbed only with tinsel, whilst others like the one on the Mar Lodge was relieved with black silk and therefore broken, all undoubtedly were designed for a purpose. In all probability they were thought to be necessary in order to flash and glitter as they twisted, turned and even sometimes rotated their way across the surface of the water. These glints or flashes of light often woke the lethargic fish out of its trance and drew its attention to the presence of the fly. Very similar to the human being, who is surveying the landscape and suddenly his attention is drawn to a specific spot by a flash of sunlight playing on a shiny stone or piece of glass, the fish, once alerted to the fly's presence, is naturally inquisitive to find out more about the fly and often that simple flash or glitter lures the fish into making that fatal mistake.

In the last two decades the famous old patterned flies of the past have largely, due to expense mainly, been superseded by hair-winged varieties, waddingtons or tube flies, although some of the plainer, smaller varieties are still dressed to specification. Far less attention is now taken of detail and in my humble opinion many of the tube flies are far too heavily dressed and often made of too stiff a variety of hair. The former fault completely obscures the body, if the tube actually has one at all and many do not, and this to my mind is a fatal mistake as it definitely reduces the effectiveness of these flies under certain conditions, although provided that the fish are alert it will still kill fish. If on the other hand the fish is either lethargic or lulled into complacency due to many other objects such as leaves, grass, etc. which are floating on the surface that day, there is little tinsel or braid visible to flash or glitter and attract the fish's attention to it, therefore it often passes over the fish unnoticed.

The latter fault of stiff hair very much reduces the life-like movement that soft hair produces as it swims through the water. Collie dog hair taken from the underside of a collie's tail, especially if this hair has a natural wave in it, is undoubtedly the best hair for dressing hair-winged flies, provided that it is not too woolly. The long winged varieties of flies such as the Collie Dog (hence its name) and the Tadpole famed as spring flies in northern rivers, are full of life-like action when tied with this hair, or alternatively fine, long hair from a goat skin. This latter hair, however, lacks the wave as it is as straight as a dye. Human hair seems least effective of all. In all probability it would seem that it is too oily and lets off tiny air bubbles. Buck tail was the most popular hair used at the beginning of the hair-wing phase of fly tying and is still used widely in the industry. This hair, however, is often difficult to obtain in the sufficient length to tie the larger sized flies, is often fairly brittle, and sometimes lacks the degree of movement that other varieties of hair have.

Tubes dressed with a top hair wing and the body left completely unobscured are to my mind by far the most effective and can be made at low cost when dressed on aluminium or brass tubes. I would, however, like to see the tube manufacturers use more imagination and produce tubes for the fly tiers in differing colours, combinations of colours, etc. to copy the bodies of the old reliable patterned flies of the past. At the moment if one wishes to use a gold or copper coloured tube the only one mass produced is a brass tube which is far too heavy at certain times of the year.

The Willie Gunn is definitely one of the best tube flies so far brought out, especially when used in spring or autumn. The man who invented this fly used a great deal of imagination by instead of inserting red, yellow and black tufts of hair and producing what might be called a red, black and yellow tube, he merely mixed up these three different coloured hairs thereby creating a well-balanced mottled wing, full of life and colour contrast, not heavily dressed, so that the thunder and lightning styled body had plenty of chance to radiate light. In essence it is a genuine attempt to latch onto the effectiveness of an old patterned fly, dressed on the tube and has been markedly successful. I only wish other fly tiers would produce tubes more closely related to the famed patterns of the past.

Tubes dressed with only a top wing could also have a throat hackle, which would also be another point of detail retrieved from the past. There is also no reason why waddington-type flies should not be dressed on similar lines and if they were I am sure the reward of success would soon increase their popularity.

Conclusions

Provided there is no one such as a ghillie with local knowledge to advise him, before an angler can make his choice of fly at the start of his day he should pay attention to the time of year, weather conditions and water conditions because these together enable him to make a rough guess as to what the water temperature might be that day. This should give him a good guide as to what size of fly to choose and also what depth his fly should be fished at, as well as the type of line to use. He must, however, be prepared to vary his fly both to the sublime and the ridiculous if his first choice proves to be ineffective. He must be prepared to vary his method of presentation if need be, rather than just flogging on for the whole day using the same fly and the same method without achieving success.

He must bear in mind both colour and type of body that the fly is made up of, according to the time of year, the clarity or turbidity of the water and the dullness or brightness of the day, before choosing the type and pattern of fly to use. On a dull day he must choose a fly which will silhouette or show up best against the sky if he is fishing a shallow fly and against the landscape or underwater bank strata if he is fishing a fly in deeper water. On a bright day, or a day of changeable light, the angler should bear the same data in mind but also choose a body that will reflect light and allow the fly to glitter or glint to alert the fish of its presence. This is particularly important when other objects such as leaves, grass, etc. are also floating on the surface. They all tend to lull the fish into complacency. Deer grass and dead leaves are often a nuisance in early spring on a windy day as they are light and brittle and easily blown into the river. Bud sheaths from deciduous trees can be a problem from mid-April to early June, and leaves are a common nuisance as they fall in the autumn.

The clarity, turbidity, peat stain of the water must be another point to consider when choosing the body or colour of fly. In turbidity and clarity a silver body seems best, whilst in peat-stained conditions gold or copper are favoured more. Colour of fly must be selected after consideration of the season and its power of contrast.

Finer points such as hackle and extreme detail in the make-up of the fly are more important in gin-clear water conditions which normally prevail in rivers early in the season and are seldom found on rivers flowing off moorland during the summer months, except in very low flows. These conditions can, however, often be found throughout the season on rivers flowing off high ground, chalk or limestone.

Having studied these aspects with care, the angler should then select a fly that he has confidence in, which roughly falls into the category that suits conditions for the day, and try a pattern in a size which suits conditions for that day. If the angler has no favourites then he should follow these tips carefully to guide him in his choice of fly.

How to Cover a Beat to Best Advantage

This depends very largely on the type of beat one is fishing on, mainly as to whether it is a beat on a large river with long, wide pools, or a beat on a small river with numerous small pools, reasonably close together. It also depends on how many rods are fishing the beat on that particular day, but in all probability this does not have much bearing on the matter, as each will have been given his own section or the rods will be fishing in pairs.

The real question that has to be answered, I think, is should an angler concentrate on fishing a small amount of water painstakingly slowly as he searches every inch of it in an immaculate manner; or should he alternatively fish a much larger amount of water quickly but thoroughly and leave himself time to go back over the entire stretch again – or certainly the best part of it? In other words, to put it in a nutshell should the angler go out in search of his fish, or should he wait for his fish to come to him, or be content with the fact that there are plenty of fish available where he is fishing and it is up to him to catch them?

Of these two schools of thought, I undoubtedly support the theory that it is best to fish lightly over a pool and then pass on to the next if I am unsuccessful, but still leaving myself time to return to cover my water for a second, or even a third time, before my allotted period expires. However, admittedly I do fish every pool down and then back up it again though generally with the same fly, this gives the fish two entirely different presentations, and it is quite extraordinary how often I catch my fish when backing up, having not been aware of moving anything as I fished the pool down. I have always been accustomed to backing up the pool again, for the simple reason that as I usually fish alone I have normally left some tackle, etc. at the head of the pool, and need to return there to collect it, and in this way no fishing time is wasted as my fly is in the water all the time.

Through experience, I believe that if there is a taking fish in the pool, he will take either as I fish down the pool or back it up. Therefore, if nothing happens I am as well to move down to the next pool. However, on my return, which may be two hours later, either the resident fish in the pool may have woken up or some fresh fish may have come into the pool in the meantime, and in both cases this gives me a better chance to catch a fish. I am certainly not, and never

will be, a believer in the theory that you can either annoy or pester fish into taking, unless of course you are continually trying something different in the way of presentation.

I will not, however, move on to another pool if fish are taking in the pool I am fishing, or if I am moving fish in it. By keeping on moving I have the chance of catching both settled or resting fish in all the other pools I fish, and also the chance of finding where a run of fish may be resting on that particular day, as well as the chance of catching more fish in the pools that I have previously fished, on my return to them.

The angler who believes in spending far more time on his pools, however, obviously fishes far less water and therefore must materially reduce his chance of finding where fish rest on that particular day, unless he is lucky enough to happen to choose to fish the one they are resting in. It would follow also that he is covering less fish and is, therefore, relying more on his skill to induce the fish in this smaller area of water to take, or hopes that fresh fish will enter these pools whilst he fishes them, and sometimes this could easily happen. On the other hand, he could so easily select a pool where there is no ready taker when he first fishes it, and there are no fresh fish coming into it and resting there. Then he must be at a disadvantage, as with continual disturbance fish can be put down, especially in lower water flows, and seldom to my mind take kindly to being continually pestered in the same fashion, whilst if the angler moved on to fresh pastures and then returned in an hour or two, it could be a very different story.

In larger rivers, where each pool might take an hour or two to fish, I still believe in fishing the water in exactly the same fashion, lightly and thoroughly down and backing it up to the head again, once I have finished fishing it down. Then either moving on to the next pool, or alternatively, if I am lucky enough to have the other side and it is on my beat then I would try my pool from a different angle first, and then move on. In my experience, provided you are continually changing your angle of presentation or mode and method of fishing, that is the very essence of success. It is monotony which the angler should try and avoid at all costs, unless of course fish are taking one method freely, then of course there is no point in altering it, but merely keep your alternatives up your sleeve for times when fish are stiff.

I am a great believer in keeping a few tricks in store, especially when the river is dropping and it looks as if fish will soon stop running, because I seriously think that if you do educate fish when they are still taking reasonably freely with everything at once, you will have nothing left in reserve for the day when they become stiff. It is, therefore, best to keep a very favoured pattern or type of fly in store which is only

Fishing white water from a vantage point

Fishing a narrow gut off a stoney outcrop

used literally when one is beaten with all others. Alternatively, keep a method such as the riffling hitch or dragged tail fly, that can and does work well at times, in reserve for the day when fish have really put their shutters up and will take no notice of other methods. Then the introduction of these 'secret weapons' cannot only do the trick and save a blank, but also be productive for several days afterwards, as these are something entirely new and unfamiliar to both the wily old retainers and the new boys alike.

Two people fishing together can be a great help to each other provided they decide on a plan of campaign, by which one fishes an entirely different size of fly to the other, or adopts a different mode or method of fishing. Then, if one is being more successful with his technique than the other, his partner can improve his chances by changing over to that method. If, however, there is no agreement between the two, they are highly likely to fish in exactly the same manner with often just a different pattern of fly. Sometimes, undoubtedly, they will be lucky, whilst otherwise they may fail through being too conservative and not being more imaginative or constructive.

At Which Side of the River to Fish

In many cases an angler does not have the choice, because he is often fishing on a single rod beat with the opposite bank being fished by another proprietor or party of tenants. It is, however, an interesting question which merits exploring.

When an angler seeks to take a fly-fishing beat as a tenant, unless he is ambidextrous and can cast equally well off either shoulder, he must be careful, if it is a single-bank beat, that he chooses a beat which suits his casting shoulder, in other words a left-hand bank for right shoulder, and a right-hand bank for left. Unless of course the beat is so open and free from casting restrictions that it makes little difference which shoulder is used, these are, however, generally few and far between.

If, however, he is lucky enough to choose and obtain a double-bank beat then naturally he has the best of both worlds, and can make his choice of which bank to fish from on the day, mainly according to weather and water conditions prevailing.

Obviously the question of which bank fishes best depends very largely on water conditions which prevail on any given day, and this can vary tremendously from pool to pool. However, the old adage of fishing from the shallow into the deep does have the biggest bearing of all on this factor. This is mainly because when you are following this golden rule, you are not only standing well away from and less likely to disturb the fish you are trying to catch in all heights of water, and especially low-water flows. Whereas in high-water flows, the fish will not be lying in the fast relentless current flowing down close to the opposite bank, but instead they will be lying in the lull on the shallow side of the stream, which once again gives the angler fishing from the shallow a tremendous advantage, certainly at the neck of the pool, and generally throughout the whole pool. In medium-water flows, however, very often both sides can have an equal advantage as fish lying to the shallow side of the current will be takeable from the deep-water side throughout the length of the pool, as well as from the shallow side.

It is quite common to find a double bank beat where in low and high water conditions the side that has the shallow side of the most pools always fishes best and has a definite advantage, whilst in medium heights there is little to choose between the two sides.

In the case of a river that does not camber to one or other side, but instead has a central current flow, more commonly found in the larger wider rivers, then often neither side has an advantage over the other. It is usual under these conditions to find that both sides use boats to enable the anglers to fish their pools to better advantage, and very often both sides (by agreement) divide the beat into an upper and lower section, and fish these sections on alternate days on a rotation system. This type of agreement generally works extremely smoothly and stops any arguments between the two fishing parties. Other types of agreement, such as fishing odd or even numbered pools on a daily rotation can also work well if the pools on these beats are reasonably close together.

On certain types of river, I have on many occasions seen the angle of light on a particular day or part of the day, favour anglers fishing from one bank far better than the other. Especially on the Lower Cassley, in medium to high water conditions favouring all the eighteen pools on the river up to the Round pool on either bank, I have several times seen the rods on one bank having a bonanza, whilst the rods on the other bank were completely blank, and vice versa, for absolutely no apparent reason, even though plenty of fish were showing. This type of happening seems to be more common on sunny days with sporadic cloud cover, but can also occur on cloudy days too.

Light can also affect pools set in deep gorges, allowing some of these pools to fish better from one side in the morning, whilst the opposite side of the same pool can be useless in the morning and excellent in the afternoon. I know others in similar situations which have never been known to have a fish caught in them after 7 p.m. in the evening even during the long period of daylight hours during June and July. Once again, I am certain these peculiarities are entirely due to light.

There is no doubt that owners or tenants who are fortunate enough to have both banks should always ensure that both sides are exploited as evenly as possible when water levels are suitable, and even sometimes when fish are stiff it pays handsomely to present one's fly to the fish from another angle by crossing to the other side, no matter how unfavourable conditions may seem from that bank.

Wind can, on occasions, create problems from one or other bank, and it is an easy way of avoiding this nuisance if one crosses to the other bank where it is then blowing from behind the angler instead of straight into his face. A little careful thought by the host on this type of day will allow him to surreptitiously end up with his weakest rods on the bank the wind favours, leaving his experienced rods to deal with the elements without unduly embarrassing anyone.

If there are no bridges or easy ways of access to the far bank of a double-bank fishery, a boat station on a wide pool about the central point of the beat can be a priceless asset. This allows anglers to be ferried too and from each bank with the least possible time wasted, as well as making it possible for an elderly or disabled person to fish from the boat if need be.

Only a few people today are probably aware of what a priceless asset the Welsh coracle was in heavily wooded sections of the river, both to fish from and for use as a ferry. This craft was so light it could be carried with ease on a man's back considerable distances up or down river, and could be launched practically at the angler's will, as it had such a shallow draught and no keel. With an expert coracle handler, every good holding lie in any pool could be fished from the best possible angle to suit the particular water height on that day, because with a couple of flicks with the paddle, the handler could position himself on either side of the current and hold the coracle in position whilst the angler tried each lie in turn. Some from one side, and others from the other. Many times when I think back on my childhood on the Welsh Dee, I wish I still had one of those marvellous craft.

Tide and Fish Movement

The importance of this aspect probably pertains more to the shorter rivers of the country or to beats on rivers sited close to the tidal estuary, but this type of information can also be usefully applied to beats some considerable distance upstream when warm water temperatures prevail during the summer months.

Obviously the timing when fish enter a salmon river viz a viz the state of tide in the estuary is of vital importance to the availability of fish in the lower beats of a salmon river. Especially when these fish are intent on running upstream with no real desire to stay in the lower pools of the river for more than a brief pause to rest, if it is necessary. However, if anglers do bother to study the daily tidal cycles they can often improve their chances of catching fish significantly, not only in the lower reaches but also many miles upstream, because they can then time the likely arrival of fresh fish entering their beat. This information should then enable them to concentrate their fishing efforts more favourably to coincide with the anticipated presence of fish in their water; albeit that many of them could well be pushing on upstream. These running fish, as we all know, are extremely difficult to catch unless they rest for a moment, and it is really in the hands of an angler to explore thoroughly his whole beat to search for the place where they are resting on the day. This may well be in the least expected places, often a tiny run or insignificant place, and seldom in a main pool. Once this place is found it is extraordinary how often a large proportion of fish running through the beat that day will use it as their halt.

Many, many times in my experience, whilst fishing a beat with several main pools and overall one to two miles in length, when fish were running through I have seen bags of ten or more killed by three or four rods in taking water of less than 10 yards in length in the one day. With no other moves anywhere on the rest of the fishable water which must have amounted to well over 1500 yards in length, including all the main holding pools, this only goes to show how easy it is to miss fish on these occasions.

Naturally, river flow does have a certain influence on when fish do actually leave the tide to enter the main river, but even in the highest of flows few leave the tide until it has reached peak flow, and most come in as the tide turns and begins to ebb, and will continue entering throughout the ebb cycle during higher water flows. When lower water flows prevail in the river, in cold water temperatures, a few may push into the lower pools and remain there, but in warmer water temperatures over 52°F there may be a significant movement off the ebb tide during the hours of darkness or in late evening, and these may well push on up river during the night. A smaller movement off the ebb tide in daylight hours can take place, but many of these fish often turn back and return to the tide to await the evening ebb when they will try again.

On narrow, long estuaries like the Kyle of Sutherland, and to a lesser extent the upper part of the Tay downstream of Perth, and the lower Tweed above Berwick, fish that are in these sections when the tide turns to flow are normally forced to turn and face the tide wherever they are at that time. Sometimes they remain stationary in that position, whereas at other times they allow themselves to drift upstream normally tail first with the tide. There is, therefore, a temporary lapse of fish entering the river over this period of the tidal cycle and at the same time an accumulation of fish building up within the estuary. These fish will be well rested by the time the flow turns to ebb and on entering the river will, in all probability, move fairly quickly through the first three miles or so, often without need of a rest, unless long stretches of rapids or broken water have to be negotiated.

The fish still at sea when the tide turns to ebb will negotiate the entire length of the estuary on the ebb and, therefore, if perchance they enter the river before the flow tide hits them, these fish will then be tired after journeying up the estuary, and many of them will need to rest shortly after they enter the river in the lower reaches.

The normal procedure is, therefore, for anglers on the lower beats to see fish tearing through their water as soon as the flow tide has peaked, but as the ebb tide recedes further fish will be more likely to begin to rest and hold in their beats for the rest of the duration of ebb tide, and until the flow tide begins; whilst the beats higher up river should benefit a few hours after high tide by which time fish that left the estuary at the top of the tide, should have reached them.

In reasonable water flows and warm water tempratures, these fish should travel at between two to three miles per hour on average, therefore, it is not difficult to make a quick calculation of their likely time of arrival in the beat you are fishing at the time. However, in cold water temperatures, in similar water flows their speed of ascent is virtually halved. In low water flows fish are likely to move into the lowest pools off the tide and often accumulate there for some time in low water temperatures, but in warm temperatures will often struggle on upstream over the shallows at night some considerable distance, even if it means having part of their back out of water over the worst watered areas. In these cases, after a fairly tortuous night of physical effort, they will rest in their new environment during daylight hours, and be fresh to move on the next night. These fish are then eminently catchable in their new habitat provided anglers use a little thought when best to employ their fishing efforts, according to the conditions that prevail.

In beats just above or actually affected by tide, it is best to fish the bottom pools just before high tide and at the turn to ebb, and then having done so, move up to the head of the beat in order to meet fish coming off the tide. Then work slowly down through the beat looking for fish which are resting; if you fish up from the bottom instead, fish can always be moving up ahead of you and, therefore, you may never catch up with them.

Fishing the Salmon Fly

When an angler is fishing a fly it is difficult to assess what is the most important factor that leads him to achieve a greater success rate.
Is it:

1. The fact the angler has confidence in the fly he is fishing with, or
2. The depth his fly is fishing at, or
3. The speed he is fishing his fly through the water, or
4. The life-like movement he is inserting into his fly by rod and handline motion.

Let us now study these points in order because in all probability it is a combination of all these that leads us to success.

1. *Is it confidence in the fly?*

There is little doubt that this does have an important bearing on an angler's success. In all probability it is merely a psychological boost to his morale but nonetheless very often has the desired effect. Most anglers have several favourite patterns that throughout their angling careers have brought them continued success, and many others have a well-battered individual fly or flies of favoured patterns which have time and time again caught fish for them, therefore, he has great faith in them. When an angler is fishing one of these favoured flies there is little doubt that he fishes with more optimism, paying greater attention and care as he covers the water to the very best of his ability, in anticipation that his lure will prove successful. If he, on the other hand, lacks this vital confidence he often fishes in a far more lackadaisical manner, often rushing over his water too quickly or missing out likely places. Even sometimes when a fish moves to his fly he misses it through lack of concentration, a thing which would have been unlikely to have happened if he had been fishing one of his trusted patterns.

I always remember an old ghillie of over fifty year's experience, on my father's beat of the Cassley, who hated to fish himself, with one of the best-taking patterned flies on that river. He knew full well how effective this pattern was and would always advise his angler to fish with it, but if you offered him a cast he would immediately change the fly for something else. Having noted this fact for many years I asked him why he would not fish that particular pattern and he wryly admitted that he had never caught a fish on it in his life and that he was never likely to as he had no faith in it. This from one of the best fly fishermen I have ever known showed how strongly he felt on the matter. I remember shortly afterwards a day when we were the only two rods on the beat, in perfect water in April 1956. We agreed that for interest we would both fish identical patterns and size of his bogey fly and that he would fish each pool in front of me. The result was that at 12.30 p.m. he had not caught a fish and I had had four beautiful springers. Absolutely frustrated he could contain himself no longer and changed his fly for a Mar Lodge and immediately killed two fish. Quite extraordinary, but in fact I have seen many, many similar cases such as that both before and since.

I myself, many years ago, decided to fish for an entire season with one pattern of fly, regardless of conditions or what river I was fishing. I chose the Mar Lodge, undoubtedly my favourite fly of the old patterns. I armed myself with every size from No. 9 upwards to 10/° and religiously kept to my plan. The end result was I killed a similar number of fish to my norm that season.

Another interesting happening was on the Oykel in late February in the 1950s. An inexperienced salmon angler, who had fished the river in early September the previous year, took a day's fishing. As it happened no fish had been killed so far that season in spite of the efforts of George Ross, the father of the manager of the Lower Oykel fishings at present. George was not previously warned that the man was coming and, therefore, by the time he found out that there was a tenant on the river it was early afternoon. The angler had set out for the Rock Pool on beat 2 in the morning, a pool where he had had success the previous year. When he arrived at the pool, although the river was high he put on a small No. 8 Brown Dog with which he had caught two fish the previous season and began fishing. George eventually arrived and out of courtesy asked the tenant if he had had any luck, and much to his surprise the angler said yes. Two fish. George's heart sank as he was sure they would be kelts but low and behold lying behind a rock, side by side, were two beautiful spring fish. When he was shown the fly they were caught on George nearly had a fit as he himself had been fishing that morning with the usual spring flies nearly ten times that size, elsewhere on the river, between 6/° and 10/° in size. Once again this plainly was an example of confidence. The angler was not sufficiently experienced to know that in the spring time you use much larger flies. Instead, he had used flies that he had killed fish on before, in the same place. Because he had confidence in them it worked, what more can be said!

2. *The depth the fly is being fished*

Once again of prime importance. Always remember that the most essential thing about fishing is for the angler to be able to present his lure where it is most clearly visible to the fish, in as natural a manner as possible.

A fish is looking through a wall of water at the lure; often this water is either turbid or peat stained so therefore it is best to try and fish one's fly against the lightest background available where fish can see it plainly silhouetted. Obviously this inevitably must be the sky, completely regardless of the water and weather conditions. Once the fly drops below what I always define as the fishes' window, the fish has to contrast the fly against a much darker background which might be rock, vegetation or moorland or even darker still, underwater rock or bank and this contrast has to be made through a wall of water as well which on occasions will be peaty or turbid, leading to a much reduced clarity of vision. The higher the fly is in the water, the more tinsel and gold and silvered bodied flies reflect the light, causing them to glint and glitter, the deeper the fly is fished in the water the less light it will reflect especially if there is any peat or turbidity in the water. Therefore the purpose of producing flies with detailed bodies is partially or completely lost once the fly is fished at an appreciable depth in these conditions.

What the angler never knows for sure is the exact depth that the fish is lying at in the pool. One thing is for sure, they very rarely lie right down on the river bed except in the shallowest pools or runs, of under 3 feet in depth. For the norm they are usually lying under half-way between the surface and the bed, unless they have been disturbed and forced to take cover. Even then they prefer to shelter under a bank or in the lull of a rock or underwater obstruction. In many cases, like an ostrich, they feel safe if their heads are hidden and they completely forget about their bodies or tails, which makes them easy prey for a poacher's snare. The angler must therefore take care that his lure is not being fished at a greater depth than the salmon itself is lying and it is undoubtedly best to err on the safe side and fish one's fly shallower rather than deeper because of this fact.

A floating line is not only much easier to cast with but also highly

Fishing the Crow's Nest with the Achness Falls in the background

effective for much of the year. It can have its drawbacks, however, in deep gorges or deep, fast stretches of water where there are normally numerous swirling surface currents and back eddies. In situations like this it is essential to sink your line underneath these into the calmer water below the surface, otherwise with a floating line snaking from eddy to eddy and being buffeted by cross currents at the same time, the angler's fly will be forced to dart about without rhyme or reason, as it follows the course of the line. This makes it look unnatural and it is, therefore, unattractive to the fish. Even a sink tip attached to the floating line rarely cures this problem. It is better, therefore, to use a double-tapered sunk line. A No. 5 King Fisher line of the past was ideal in these situations. High water conditions, in fast flowing pools, can also create similar problems, and these can cause the fly to skate on the surface of the water when it is being fished on a floating line. Floating lines are, under normal conditions, an essential part of fly fishing during the summer period once the water temperature rises above 48°F. Seemingly, under these conditions unless the river is in spate or flowing at a high level, fish tend to be far more attracted to a fly fished close to the surface than one fished at a greater depth. There is also no doubt that sometimes under these conditions, a difference of 2 to 3 inches in the depth that the fly is fished at can be critical and can make the difference between a blank day and a bonanza. I have often seen the difference in depth between the tail-fly fishing and that which the dropper was fishing at making all the difference; on one day all the fish would come to the dropper and on the other to the tail fly, even though both flies were identical in pattern and size.

Anglers should be more careful when fishing a floating line as to the weight of the actual fly they are fishing, and should adjust the length of their cast accordingly, in order to make sure the weight of the fly does not either cause the point of the line to sink, or else itself submerge too far under the surface. This is particularly necessary when Esmond Drury hooks are being used.

Finally, always remember if one can entice a fish to travel a distance to one's fly it will be travelling at an increased impetus, as it is totally committed, when it takes the fly. Therefore, there is a far better chance of hooking it securely. If the fly is high on the surface of the water this usually happens, but the deeper one fishes, the closer the fly is to the fish, so the more the speed of movement towards the fly is reduced when the fish takes. This often leads to a snatch or pluck rather than a solid take as the fish almost warily noses the fly.

153

A firm stance to aid casting power

Using a long rod to dibble the edge of the current

3. *Is it the speed of the fly?*

As I have said before on previous pages, this is certainly an important factor which in most cases an angler is partially able to control, provided he is fishing with a sufficiently long enough rod to do so. If he has too short a rod, however, it is the current flow of the river which will control the speed of swing, as the fly traverses the width of the river on all but the narrowest of pools.

I personally believe that it is absolutely essential to allow fish that are lying close to where the fly lands, to see the fly clearly before it moves away from them. Therefore, as I have described before, I make the fly hesitate for a reasonable moment of time before allowing it to move away from the fish in question. I am also positive it is advantageous to con the fish into thinking that the fly is trying to escape from him, as this, in my opinion, makes fish far more positive in their action as they actually make contact with the fly and normally results in a solid take which embeds the barb of the hook. I therefore tend to handline quickly in order to create this effect rather than lead the fly away from them with my rod tip. This is mainly because the latter can result in too much force being inserted on the line by the current velocity which can over-exaggerate this action, and in order to reduce this risk I keep my rod angled square to the current.

This angle of rod tip enables me to control to a high degree the speed at which my fly traverses the width of the pool and at the same time allows me to hang it over likely taking places causing it to pause, once again, to allow fish in these lies to get a good look at it before allowing it to continue on its journey.

When an angler is fishing with a floating line in the authentic manner, and not trying to fish the true grease-line method, he will find that with his rod tip angled square to the current any fear of his fly skating on top of the water is much reduced. The fly skidding on top of the water can often cause problems in fast, streamy necks of pools or fast runs, and although mending the line does tend to check it I believe my alternative method is more effective. Mainly because the speed the fly is fishing at is checked and controlled throughout the entire traverse of the fly across the pool whereas mending the line only checks the speed temporarily, and has to be repeated.

In the spring and autumn salmon usually favour a faster moving fly than they do during the summer months, when water temperatures are on the whole much higher and fish are accordingly more lethargic. It is during the autumn and spring months that a fairly fast handlining action by the angler often pays handsome dividends. Similarly,

The Round Pool Pot and the Round Pool

at these times of year the backing up method can be ideally suited for this purpose, when wind ruffles the stiller areas of pools, or as an alternative method of presentation in normal conditions. There is little doubt that fewer fish are lost when an angler is backing up a pool, mainly because the line between the angler and his fly is bound to be taut as the angler is always moving upstream against the current. Therefore, there is inevitably a better penetration of his hooks when the impact of the take occurs. In the summer months I have always found it pays to move the fly in very short draws mainly in order to keep absolute contact with the fly and not for the sole purpose of putting movement into it. Fish are far more lackadaisical at this time of year especially in low water flows when water temperatures are high, and in those conditions tend to move far more quietly when taking. However, even during the summer period, backing up can still be a very effective way of fishing a pool, but when this method is used at this time of year it must be fished at a snail's pace both concerning the angler's movement upstream and the speed of handline action, compared with the faster speed used in spring and autumn. When using Wood's authentic grease-line method, which is most effective during the summer months, the fly must be allowed literally to hang inert in the current. The angler must, therefore, allow no drag on his line or movement of his line, and must negate these actions by continually mending his line so that it lies parallel to the current flow.

4. *Is it the movement of the fly?*

I think it is obvious to most fishermen that regardless of what bait or lure he is trying to tempt his quarry with, one of the most basic requirements to assure success is to be able to present his lure in the most natural way possible, in order to simulate the actions of what his lure or bait is meant to imitate. In the case of the fly fisherman, when he is using the larger sizes of fly there is no doubt he is trying to imitate small fish or elvers, and in the case of the smaller sizes of fly, either tiny fish or water-borne invertebrates. When he is using the authentic grease-line method as advocated by Wood, undoubtedly he is trying to imitate plankton, a vegetation which merely hangs inert in the current, hence the whole theory of this method of fly fishing, which preaches that no movement or drag must be allowed to be transmitted to the fly. Therefore, continual mending of the line to keep it parallel to the flow of the current is absolutely necessary to allow the fly to hang inert. It is also necessary in this case, to fish with a fly which is drab in colour to match the colouring of this natural vegetation.

When an angler is trying to imitate a small fish or elver, he should simulate the swimming motion of these creatures, altering the speed of its movement, allowing it to pause and then quicken pace and even hang for a moment. All these actions allow life-like motions to be transmitted to the fly as well as allowing the actual dressing of the fly itself to move in a life-like fashion. If the fly is allowed to quiver, quicken pace, dart, slow down and briefly pause, these hesitant actions all enable the varied hackles either to fluff out or shut, whilst the hair or feathered wings quiver and tremble and the bodies scintillate light. This naturally helps to give the actual fly a life-like appearance, and makes it come to life, whereas it would otherwise be swept round by the pace of the current with hackle shut, wing flat and lacking lustre, and the body often shielded.

I well remember a famed old patterned fly, the Golden Eagle. This fly had a very pronounced down throat hackle almost as long as the wing. One day when I was fishing this fly on a short line in a narrow gorge, and was therefore able to watch it visually as it traversed the pool, I first realised the importance of this hackle regarding the attractiveness of the fly. After every upstream movement, the fly hesitated and the hackle puffed out giving the fly a most life-like action. There is little doubt that this is why fish were fatally attracted to it, as time and time again this fly killed fish when all else failed.

When fishing with tiny flies, the angler who wishes to imitate water-borne invertebrates instead of fish, should work his flies in quick, erratic, short bursts. This, once again, allows the hackle and detailed dressings on his fly time to flex and bring life into the fly, and at the same time imitates the natural actions of these invertebrates.

All too often in my opinion, the angler allows his fly to fish at the same monotonous speed without any regard to what it is meant to simulate. This, therefore, prevents the detailed dressing of the fly, which is there for a purpose, from having a chance to prove itself.

Only when the angler is either dibbling or dragging one of his flies on the surface can it really be considered that he is trying to imitate a fly. Then it is one which has been blown onto the surface of the water, and is struggling to save itself from drowning and very effective these differing methods can be.